# I Just Lost 20 Pounds

# Pounds

A Permanent Weight Loss Solution

Lisa Airhart

ISBN: 978 057 872 091 3

Published 2020

DISCLAIMER

To my husband, Michael, my biggest supporter throughout my journey. Thank you for your undying patience and love. I am truly blessed.

# Table of Contents

# Chapter 1: The Battle

*"In the middle of conflict lies opportunity."*

- Albert Einstein

*Look! There it is again.* Stephanie peered through her kitchen window and spotted a vibrant colored, male cardinal perched on a branch in the hemlock trees. The cardinal sang, as if to say "Good morning" directly to her. Stephanie was often busy in the morning, getting herself ready for work and sending her girls off to school, but she couldn't miss the sight of the brilliant, red colored bird perched among the deep green branches. The cardinal could capture anyone's attention, even if it was just for a moment.

Let me tell you Stephanie's story. Stephanie, a forty-eight-year-old schoolteacher, lived in Portland, Maine. She lived there with her twin teenage daughters and her husband. She grew up in Massachusetts, just north of Boston, with her parents and sister, Meg. From there, Stephanie went to college, where she met her husband of twenty years. Everything went as planned – the house, husband, kids, and dog. She lived her life like most of her friends did; they were in each other's weddings and pretty much had children around the same time, too.

Stephanie took some time off from teaching when her children were small. She loved being home with her girls. It worked for her. She took them to the weekly storytime at the local library. They would regularly visit the Children's Museum. She would arrange playdates for her daughters with children from the neighborhood. She was content being a stay-at-home mom.

When the twins were ready for kindergarten, Stephanie and her husband decided it was time for her to go back to work. The couple just bought a bigger house and bills needed to get paid. The opportunity came up for a job as a fourth-grade teacher at a local school, so Stephanie quickly applied, knowing convenient jobs like this were hard to come by. To her surprise, Stephanie was offered the job. That's when the fun began – balancing family and work. Stephanie drove her children to and from activities, showed up at school events, hosted the holidays at their home, and occasionally snuck date nights with her husband. Her carefree life soon turned into a whirlwind of running from one event to the next. She found it hard to find time for herself with her busy schedule. When she did make time, it was to gather at a neighbor's house for gossip, cocktails, cheese, and crackers. This is what she looked forward to at the end of the week to cope with the stress. As the years went by, Stephanie noticed the number on the scale increasing and her clothes becoming tight-fitting. She was gradually becoming uncomfortable with her body image. She began hiding behind baggy clothes and large jewelry. Stephanie was always fit, so a twenty-plus gain was quite noticeable. She became self-conscious and began to feel unattractive. Not only was Stephanie aware of her weight gain, but she also felt that she didn't have the energy she once had. She felt like a zombie just getting through the day. She often had to hit the snooze button at least twice before getting out of bed. This went on for years.

Stephanie tried fighting back. Over the years she faced an ongoing battle with the latest diets. First, Stephanie tried the Atkins diet; she quickly lost ten pounds, however the fresh sourdough bread at her local market continued to be enticing. Then came the Zone diet. Specifics of this diet include eating in a 1-2-3 ratio: 1 gram of fat to 2 grams of protein to 3 grams of carbohydrates. This diet also recommends a regular eating schedule. Stephanie figured the specificity of this diet would work for her, but she found this to be untrue when both the girls came down with the flu, which resulted in Stephanie eating crackers and drinking ginger ale. Stephanie's neighbor, Bev, was successful on the gluten-free diet, so Stephanie thought she would try that. She thought that diet might help because of her neighbor's support, but Stephanie didn't need to be on the gluten-free diet since she wasn't allergic or sensitive to gluten, so she became bored with it. Lastly, Stephanie found the Keto diet, which promises weight loss, but she struggled staying on it through the holiday season – just too much red wine and Christmas cookies. Her frustration with all of this made her turn to exercise, thinking that would do the trick. She was athletic in high school, and an exercise regimen seemed to work for her sister, who was a runner. However, it didn't work for Stephanie; she didn't like running, even with the song "Stronger" by Kelly Clarkson playing while she ran. A more fitting song soon turned into "Another One Bites the Dust." Stephanie felt defeated. Running wasn't going to work for her, as it had when she was in college and could run for miles. Stephanie wasn't going down easily; she gathered her friends to go walking with her. Even though being in the fresh air always made Stephanie feel better, the walks were never consistent – they only happened when the three of them could get together, which was a challenge with their busy schedules. Stephanie started to feel grumpy and others around her noticed. *Come on,* Stephanie thought; she didn't want to look like Miss America, she just wanted to feel healthy so she could be energized to keep up with the demands of her busy life. Was that too much to ask? No!

One day, Stephanie went to her mailbox, and there it was – a wedding invitation! Stephanie knew it was coming because her dear niece, Kayla, was getting married in the spring. Now Stephanie was really motivated. After all, her whole family would be at Kayla's wedding and Stephanie did not want to be the "overweight sister" at the gathering. You see, Stephanie's older sister, the runner, could do no wrong. Meg still somehow maintained her high school weight, had a beautiful house, and kept up with her three busy children. Meg didn't need to work – her husband had a lucrative salary. Meg enjoyed her job so she chose to work part time as an acupuncturist, unlike Stephanie, who had to go back to work. Meg's job allowed her the luxury to make her own hours and she was never pressured to produce an income to pay the bills. It appeared to Stephanie that Meg had it all together, and she was beginning to feel envious.

Stephanie knew she needed a different approach to weight loss this time around. She was not going to press the replay button again and again, but what was she going to do? How was she going to be successful this time? One evening, Stephanie and her neighborhood friends gathered at her house for a "moms' night." The perpetual conversation about the "diet" resurfaced. However, Stephanie seemed to be the only one serious about finding a solution; the others just happily sipped their glasses of sauvignon blanc and joked about it. Because of the upcoming wedding, however, Stephanie had a sense of urgency the others didn't have. She didn't want to show up at the family wedding feeling self-conscious about her weight gain. Stephanie attempted to wash her worries down with each sip of wine. Seeing how distraught Stephanie was, her friend chimed in, "My cousin had success keeping her weight off by hiring a health coach who specializes in weight loss." Stephanie heard this and was on full alert – this was the answer she was searching for! A coach! Someone to hold her hand through the process. Stephanie knew she needed the phone number of that health coach – immediately. She just had to lose twenty pounds for the wedding! Instantly, cell phones came out and phone numbers were exchanged. Stephanie knew she had to make the call.

Suddenly, Stephanie's neighbor cried, "Hey, did you see that?"

"He's back!" Stephanie exclaimed, "I saw him last week when I was getting ready for work."

From the picture window, Stephanie's friends could see a cardinal fly into the hemlock trees again, fluttering its wings, as if applauding and saying, "Right on, lady."

And so, the journey began.

# Chapter 2: I've Been in Your Shoes

*"We cannot become who we need to by remaining what we are."*

– Oprah Winfrey

Does any of Stephanie's story sound familiar to your own story? Have you told yourself the lie that you are not disciplined enough to be free from weight-loss issues? Is your head buzzing with thoughts of how to conquer the problem, but you don't know where to turn next? Do you walk around pretending it doesn't bother you when it really does? Are your self-defeating thoughts interfering with relationships with your family and friends? Are you like Stephanie and are WAITING for the weight to come off before you release your full potential and step into your true self? I'm here to tell you that you are not alone – there are millions of women struggling with the same debilitating thoughts of feeling ashamed, guilty, and disappointed.

Well, friend, I've been in Stephanie's shoes, and since you are reading this book, I know you have too! Like Stephanie, I was able to lose weight, but had a hard time maintaining the weight loss. I want to share my story with you. Growing up in suburbia in the seventies was a wonderful experience. In the summer, we would go outside, walk to friends' houses, ring their doorbells, and ask if they wanted to come outside and play. We were always swinging on the swing sets, jumping rope, or riding our bikes around the block. It was the natural thing to do back then. Lunch was probably a grilled cheese or peanut butter and jelly sandwich. I don't remember wanting to come inside for lunch, because my friends and I lost track of time; we were too engaged in whatever game we invented. Instead, we came in for lunch because one of our parents called us. Unless it was a well-planned picnic, eating just got in the way of our fun.

At night, when the ice cream truck came down the street with its bells ringing, the kids from the neighborhood stopped what they were doing to bolt and find its location; there was no need for a GPS. We didn't necessarily run for the truck because we craved the ice cream; we found the ice cream truck for the fun of putting the fudge part of the chocolate éclair we just purchased against our lips, pretending it was lipstick. We'd always get a chuckle out of it.

When I look back, I realize we were all so skinny. I don't remember ever being tired or running out of energy. We laughed, we joked, and we jumped in the neighbor's pool. If we were thirsty, we drank water from the backyard hose, letting it run for a minute until the water was cold. I'm sure we sprayed one another, too. Those were some good times and I will never forget them. We lived in the moment; food wasn't our vice because it came in second after we fed ourselves with laughter, friendship, and some imagination.

Time doesn't wait for anybody – we grew up, went to college, found careers, got married, and had children. A lot changed since we were kids; communication, conveniences, and daily demands pulled us away from the simple, carefree childhood we once had.

What was once not on my radar soon appeared: weight gain. It is easy to put your needs last when you have a family to care for and a career to pay attention to

– it happens. I was busy and at first didn't even notice the change in my body. Looking back, I was in denial. I was really good at making excuses like, *"Oh, I'm not gaining weight, I'm just bloated because I have my period,"* or *"I'm looking into a 'fat mirror' – that's not really how I look."* I just kept on telling myself these lies. It really hit me when I walked into a clothing store and could only fit into a pair of pants two sizes larger than I was used to wearing. I refused to buy them; I actually spent hours looking for jeans that would fit me in the size I was accustomed to wearing. I searched until I found a company that sized their jeans differently. Apparently the store's marketing plan was successful. I know this was shallow thinking, but it worked for me back then. It sounds crazy, right? I knew I had to get a handle on my weight. I couldn't let it take over my life. I just kept thinking, *When I lose weight, I will have control of my life again. I'll be happier and have more energy. Weight loss is the solution, the cure.* Another realization surfaced when I was looking at a passport photo I had taken for an upcoming trip. It was not the best lighting and I'm pretty sure they didn't get my good side, but I remember looking at it and passing it off as someone else. *That can't be me in the picture*, I thought, but it was. I remember saying, "Why do I look so old?" When you're five feet and one inch, like me, you gain weight in your cheeks – the ones on your face. "Oh boy," I said. The person looking at me in the passport picture didn't align with who I was inside. I knew that for sure. I held on to that thought. Does this sound familiar to you?

On the outside it looked like everything was fine, but on the inside it wasn't. There was inner turmoil. I was anxious and insecure. I believed I was just not "good enough." No matter how hard I worked at it, I just couldn't keep up. I was floundering both at work and at home. I felt ugly and lonely and secretly went through bouts of depression. I did seek help through therapy, but it seemed more of a chore to attend a session and there were never any lasting changes. I seemed to end up right where I began. My refuge became food and wine. I secretly would snack on potato chips and Ben & Jerry's ice cream. I just wanted to get off the hamster wheel but wasn't sure how. I was confused. I was doing everything right – so I thought. I worked hard, prepared homemade meals, had a career, drove my daughter to her activities, attended church most Sundays. It just wasn't working. So

I thought my cure would be regular exercise and a proper diet. This is what I knew at the time.

Over the years I tried diets, but they didn't have long-lasting results. Yes, cutting down on carbohydrates did work for me, but I'm Italian – I love bread and pasta! Not having those would be like cutting off my right arm. Maybe I'm being a little dramatic, but you get the point. I tried joining a gym and I took classes that I disliked. Yup, when I pulled up to the gym, I would saunter to the door with my head down, knowing what the next sixty minutes would be like. I continued to go back to the gym because I thought *no pain, no gain.* I was always athletic and competitive, so this was a hard exercise motto to forget. Oh, I had a lot to learn. I don't mind exercising, but I don't want it to be demanding. Exercise for me became both emotionally and physically exhausting and the lack of consistency just made me feel like a failure. The next years I spent up and down the diet and exercise roller coaster. Up and down, round and round I went. Remember what Einstein said about doing the same thing over and over again and expecting a different result. Yeah – insanity! Still, I didn't give up the thought that one day I would look and feel better. I began to realize that I had to reframe my thinking and take action. Deep down, I felt there was a solution, but it obviously wasn't what I was doing. I began to research. I became committed to finding a solution. I started to read books on spirituality, personal growth, and health by leaders in the field such as Louise Hay, Dr. Wayne Dyer, Dr. Andrew Weil, Gabrielle Bernstein, Deepak Chopra, Gay Hendricks, and Brendon Burchard. I listened to podcasts, practiced yoga, and meditated. I knew myself, after all – I was determined to find a solution. I was getting closer to the answer.

Suddenly, just like what happened for Stephanie, the missing link appeared. I remember sitting alone outside one summer afternoon on my backyard patio. I was pondering at the time what I was going to do to fill "the void." The void was the scary thought of my daughter soon going off to college and becoming more independent, and my being faced with empty nest syndrome. I could no longer hide behind the excuse "I can't do that right now, my daughter needs me." Well, this excuse was soon vanishing, and I was beginning to worry. Yes, I have a loving husband, a good career, and a friendly dog, but I love being a mom – the thought of Sophia going out of state to school was bittersweet. For me it was the realization that I had to face the truth: I had to do something, or I was going to eat and drink my way through the next decade. Just then my answer popped up on my computer screen – I received an email about becoming a certified health coach. I looked closer, and the email definitely caught my attention. I read on; the email was generated from Gabrielle Bernstein, a reliable source. *Hmm*, I thought. *Let me Google the school to see what this is all about.* I don't just act on an invitation that appears on my screen. I began to research The Institute of Integrated Nutrition. I loved the school's mission – it directly aligned to my new beliefs. It felt right, and the timing was perfect. I eagerly signed up for the course. I knew it! There is so much more to being healthy than eating salad every day and running for miles down the street. This put it all together for me. It was the final piece of the puzzle I was looking for. My transformation began!

I lost the unwanted pounds and most importantly learned how to maintain it. Most diets don't do this – they get you there, but don't keep you there. It's actually much easier than you think. I basically eat what I want and look forward to the exercise that I do. No guilt, no shame!

What I had to learn was to make some well-needed lifestyle changes.

I have to tell you, I truly enjoyed going through my closet and giving away clothes that did not fit. Those larger clothes no longer served me. It was the ultimate reward to go out and buy a pair of size six jeans – there was no more hiding and pretending. This is who I am. There is no going back. For me, it was a rite of passage. This journey became more than just weight loss; it was life changing! I did it, and I know you can do it too!

This is a book about losing unwanted pounds and maintaining your weight loss so you are your best self. I want to clarify that "slender" does not necessarily mean healthy and is not the goal. Your ideal weight – the weight at which you feel your best and one that you can maintain safely – is not a specific number on a scale that is the same for everyone. Your optimal weight is unique for your particular body type, age, and genetics. Rather, this book is about creating a healthy relationship with food and a balanced lifestyle that allows you to feel good. Know you can be happy with your body and put being overweight behind you. This approach worked for me, and I want to share it with you. So let's begin to make you feel good again!

# Chapter 3: There Is a Way

*"Always remember you are absolutely unique, just like everybody else."*

– Margaret Mead

You're probably wondering how this is all going to work. After all, you've tried the latest diets, and I'm willing to bet you are already familiar with eating healthy. You might even exercise regularly, and you are still frustrated that you are not getting the results you're looking for. You are asking yourself, "How is this approach different?" Well, it is unique because this is a holistic approach to weight loss. It incorporates the mental, physical, and spiritual components of being healthy and maintaining your ideal weight. The book can be broken down into four areas. The first step is to get into alignment with the body you desire. You have to feel it, act it, and visualize it. Next, you will learn how to take care of yourself with your physical world through sleep, nutrition, and exercise. Thirdly, you will dive deeper into your lifestyle to become aware of where you need a little more tender loving care. The last part of the book is focused on your inner world – spirit and self-care.

Chapter 4 is a fundamental step and where the process begins. You will get real and connect to the reason you are showing up for this transformation. You will get clear about what you desire, hope, and dream. Do not skip this step! In this chapter, the purpose is to be in alignment with your goals. What you focus on is what you intend to bring about in life. This is done before you take action toward your desired outcome.

Yes, nutrition and exercise do have a place, but your weight-loss success is not about how much willpower you have or how disciplined you are. This is covered in Chapters 6 and 7. In this book, you will learn to make healthy food choices that work for you and find physical activity that fits your lifestyle. Often, people talk about what they "should" or "shouldn't" be doing to diet and exercise – making statements like, "I shouldn't be eating out all the time," or "I should have gone to the exercise class this morning." Perfection is not the goal here, as it will only discourage you from moving forward. Instead, this is about enjoying the process and making small steps that add up to big changes.

We are busier than ever. Not only is *what* you eat important, but it is also *how* you eat. Let's face it: a lot of us eat on the go, rushing through meals to get to our next task. In this book, you will learn how to cultivate an awareness around food through mindful eating.

Your lifestyle has an enormous effect on your well-being. In Chapters 8 through 11, you will reflect on how you are doing in the areas of home environment, finances, relationships, and career. Where might you need to bring balance into your life? Many aspects of our life fuel us besides food. This concept reminds me of an episode of the HBO hit series *Sex and the City* when the main character, Carrie, purchased a *Vogue* magazine instead of food when she was hungry because she felt *it fed her more*. I ask you: is your current home environment comfortable and a place to relax? Do you have control over your finances or is it the other way around? What is the current state of your close relationships? Do you spend time with people who support you? Are you where you want to be in terms of your career?

Let's face it, being out of balance in one of these areas can be stressful. As you know, if prolonged, stress wreaks havoc on the body. Whatever stress you face, either from relationships, careers, environment, or finances, affects your body. When the stressor never relents, the same process keeps continuing, over and over, in your body. Your cortisol levels increase, causing you to store fat, and, in turn, making you vulnerable to weight gain. Additionally, when you are in a stressful situation, you may not make the best food choices; your hunger cues are interrupted, causing you to overeat. This is why it is essential to approach weight loss with a holistic approach. In this book, you will learn how to manage areas of your life that could cause you stress and interfere with your weight reduction. Don't get me wrong – a little stress is actually healthy. Stress helps the body prepare to take action. For example, stress keeps you alert when you drive at night and feel tired. If someone suddenly cuts you off, your brain will send you the signal to take action and put your foot on the brake. The stress I'm talking about is prolonged periods of time when your body does not return to homeostasis or its natural state.

Chapters 12 and 13 focus on your inner world through spirituality and self-care. Basically, the practice of self-care is integrated throughout this book. Eating nutritious foods, getting proper sleep, and exercising are all part of self-care. Chapter 13 talks about intentionally incorporating it into our lives because it can easily be overlooked. Spirituality, like self-care, encourages introspection. It's bringing about wholeness. Spirituality as seen in this book offers the clarity and comfort often needed when going through a transformation.

Every person is unique. As the quote at the beginning of the chapter reminds us, this uniqueness is one of the beauties in life – we are different. Diets are not one-size-fits-all. You have to take into account things like gender, ethnic background, age, seasons, and genetics. No one way of eating works for everyone and no one type of exercising works for everyone. Additionally, no one person needs the same self-care as the next. The crucial part of successful weight loss is to find what works for you. It's about remaining flexible and knowing that your needs change over time. The fact that you've picked up this book tells me you are surrendering to the idea that you know there is a way. Congratulations! This certainly is not a book about being skinny; it's about making a connection to what makes *you* feel good. Only you know the answer.

In this book, you will become aware of how the mind, body, and spirit work in conjunction with one another, guiding you to good health and optimal weight. There is a lot of information being presented to you – I wanted you to see the big picture. Intuitively you will take from it what you need to create a permanent transformation for yourself.

# Chapter 4: Ask and You Shall Receive

*"If you can dream it, you can do it."*

– Walt Disney

## Dream

Your goal begins with a dream, and the mind has no limitations. This is why we fly airplanes and can travel long distances – thank you, Orville and Wilbur Wright. Inventors' dreams led us to communicate via phones and not through the Pony Express – thank you, Alexander Graham Bell. It all starts with a thought, which turns into a dream, and your dream becomes your goal. This thought is yours – all yours. This goal excites you, connects with you, and makes you smile.

Set your compass and push aside all the negative chatter standing in the way. You may come across thoughts along the lines of: *I'm too old*; *I already tried this before, and it didn't work*; *I take after my father and he had trouble with weight loss*; *I just don't have what it takes*; *I'll try it, but it won't last.* These thoughts creep up and deter us from our goals. Push these thoughts aside.

As a kid growing up in Rhode Island, I spent the summer riding my bike all around the neighborhood, over and over again and around the block. My friends and I entertained ourselves by dreaming. We pretended our bikes were actually cars – mine was a Porsche; my friend Anne's was a Corvette. We talked about living in a mansion, and, of course, our husbands were the latest celebrities on television. My point is, it is natural to dream big. Kids do it all the time, so why do we have to stop as adults? Dreaming is about anticipating the future. It's fun! You have permission to be whatever you want and live however you want to live. As it turns out, my childhood dreams were not just a pastime – I love my house, my husband is a prince, and I drive a nice car.

## Identify the "Why?"

The approach to weight loss in this book is unique – it goes beyond dieting and demanding exercise routines. Furthermore, you are going to be taught a holistic approach to weight loss that includes your mind, body, and soul. In doing so, you first need to make the connection to WHY you want to lose weight. Do not overlook this vital step. By establishing the reason why you want to lose weight, you are connecting to your soul and spirit's deepest desire. It's where you create your thoughts, visions, and actions. You want to think about what really fills you up rather than consume satisfaction from just the external world. For instance, if you are just jumping on the weight-loss bandwagon because it's a New Year's resolution or because your colleagues or friends are on a diet program, you haven't a made a connection to your purpose. Chances are you will be soon falling off the same bandwagon within a few months. Conversely, if you are aligned to the inner world, your spirit, then the desire comes from within and you will stay on course and succeed. This is true because your inner world is where your true power lies. To find your answer, you have to quiet the mind and focus inward. You do this by creating space and getting grounded. Either settle down in your "happy place" – the beach, a park, your backyard – or use a more formal approach through meditation and prayer. Even when I didn't know how to meditate, my answers appeared by simply slowing down and quieting the mind. In my junior year of college, I traveled with a friend to Daytona Beach in Florida. This was a well-needed vacation because I was on the go seven days a week between being a full-time college student and working two jobs to pay for it. It was my spring semester of my junior year. *Oh boy,* I thought to myself. *What am I going to do with the rest of my life?* I was a psychology major, but I knew I did not want to become a therapist, counselor, or psychologist. I remember sitting in a lounge chair, basking in the afternoon sun and staring at the crashing waves. I finally felt relaxed and rested, enjoying the idyllic beach. I was still and in my happy place. Voila! Here in this calm, quiet setting, my question was answered – a teacher! It felt right. Now, the teaching profession consumes my family. You see, I have aunts, uncles, cousins, and my very own father who was a teacher, but I had to travel to Daytona Beach to figure it out. I'm convinced God has a sense of humor. So when I returned from my trip, I did my research and talked to an academic advisor and figured out a way to make this happen. I completed my undergraduate degree at Rhode Island College. From there, I entered the Masters of Education Program at Lesley University in Boston. My friends, the answer will come when you create the space for it!

Now, you might be saying you need to make a change for an immediate purpose like an upcoming event, such as fitting into a bikini for your spring vacation to Aruba or fitting into your favorite dress for your twenty-fifth high school reunion. This is a connection to your outer world – still motivating, to say the least. There is nothing wrong with those reasons, but I want you to look further and dig deeper. Go beyond the ego and ponder how others around you will benefit. Go within, connect with your authentic self. You're here to maintain the weight loss! Perhaps you want to have more energy when you're playing with your kids or grandkids because it brings you so much joy and you want to be actively involved in their lives. Maybe you want to be able to participate in a 5K race with the girls from work to benefit a local animal shelter because you are an animal advocate. You have a burning desire for animals to exist without fear or abuse. Your purpose may be that you want to inspire others you love to live a happy, healthy life. You've seen too many of your loved ones live a life of worry and fear. The reason why will surely benefit others. If you don't have a true understanding of why you want to lose weight you will soon find yourself bored and frustrated, and you may want to quit. The more feelings you have connected to what you want, the more commitment you will have to stay on course. Get excited about your purpose! This is your true goal – not the number on the scale. Trust that your desire for change is showing up in your life for a reason and the timing is perfect.

## Create the Vision

To get to your optimal weight, you are going to have to say goodbye to the body you're in. Your body will change; it served you well at the time, but it's time for the transition. Get comfortable with the change. You will realize your body is different when you replace old clothes with new outfits. You are going to look different – accept it. This may sound silly, but often people who lose weight still see themselves as heavy. Their body has adjusted but their mind has stayed with what is familiar. I'm saying to make the transformation in your mind first, and your body will follow. You have believe it, then you will see it – not the other way around. Welcome this physical change with open arms.

Give yourself the time and the freedom to visualize your future. Take a moment, sit quietly, close your eyes, and picture your weight loss as if it already happened. How do you see yourself in your new body? Envision your desired body shape. What will it feel like when you walk in a room? Imagine the clothes you would wear and how they will look on you. Feel excited knowing you made the shift. You are doing this for yourself. Love yourself where you are. You must feel good now, not two months from now. Open your eyes and know that it already happened.

Now that you can imagine your transformation and know the reason why it is so important to you at this time in your life to lose the weight, take it a step further and create a vision board to remind you of your dreams. On the vision board, include what you will be doing once you are successful. Doing so yields success because what you focus on expands. A vision board is a collage of images, pictures, and affirmations of your desires. Remember, you've identified why, so now you will be able to visually look at your board to keep your ideas alive. The purpose of a vision board is to serve as a source of inspiration, focus, and motivation. To complete this, you can make a poster board with pictures, or you can simply create one on Pinterest. Any size you choose will suffice, so have fun and be creative! Believe what you want to achieve as if your goal has already been actualized. This is the whole purpose why it is so important to identify why you want to lose weight. You need to have a specific purpose that resonates with you. I am here to tell you that you are worthy of living a healthy, fulfilling, and happy life. Believe this is so!

Just by starting to take action, you have committed to your cause. If you feel the desire, the seed has been planted. Trust me, you have what it takes to get there, or you wouldn't have dreamed it to be possible; you just have to keep focused on your goal. You get to your goal step by step. When I think about this process, I often admire ornate public buildings. I take a moment and marvel at the beauty and hard work that went into constructing such a building. Someone's vision made it happen, just like your vision makes your dreams happen – brick by brick. It's normal to question yourself and wonder if you are doing things correctly. However, just keep focused; there will be doubts and distractions. Let the thoughts come and go. Combatting the moments of confusion or doubt is the reason why you developed your vision board in the first place – to maintain focus and not get sidetracked. Get excited about the positive change in well-being you are going to experience. You can now visualize what you will look like and how you will feel, so get comfortable with your new look. It's who you were meant to be. This is the first step in your journey to permanent weight loss – visualizing the result and believing it as if it has already happened.

## Set Your Goal

Now that you've established a clear image and reason why it's important to you, it's time to take action. You will have to make some changes in your outer world in order to see results. You may want to create a "SMART" goal, an individualized statement created to direct you toward completing your goal and achieving lasting change. The SMART acronym stands for specific, measurable, attainable, relevant, and time-bound. Now, how do you actually use this acronym? Let's take a closer look.

### Specific

You want your goal to be simple. Start with an objective that is specific and clearly defined, such as, "I will lose ten pounds by walking briskly for thirty minutes a day, five days a week." What you don't want is to be vague by saying, "I want to lose weight."

**Measurable**

Make sure your goal is measurable. As you work toward your goal, track your progress. For example, "I will lose 1.5 pounds per week."

**Attainable**

The SMART goal needs to be attainable and realistic. You want to be successful, so choose a goal you can reach. If your goal isn't realistic, you can make adjustments. For example, instead of losing 1.5 pounds a week, maybe aiming for losing one pound a week will work better. Lasting change takes time. It won't happen overnight. The idea is to be successful.

**Relevant**

Your goal must have meaning to you, and only you. Own your dream! This goes back to the reason why you want to lose weight that we looked at earlier. Your goal has to matter in your life.

**Time-bound**

Your goal also needs a target date. Choose a time frame that allows you enough time to accomplish your goal but is not too far off in the distance that you lose your motivation. In the example of losing 1.5 pounds a week, it would take just about seven weeks to reach the goal of losing ten pounds. Having a deadline will hold you accountable.

After you complete your first goal, you can then go ahead and add another goal. Look at your current habits and choose one you want to change. As you read this book, you will be presented with suggestions that could be used to create your own personal SMART goals. By using the SMART goal strategy you are breaking down the process into bite-size pieces that are easy to swallow. Remember: slow and steady wins the race!

Don't forget to reward yourself when you obtain your goal. Reward follows effort. Celebrate your accomplishment! This can be done by intentionally setting aside time in the middle of the day to read a good book or scheduling an appointment for a full-body massage. Either way, it's important to recognize your victories so you can keep the momentum going.

# Chapter 5: Sweet Dreams

*"Sleep is the best meditation."*

– Dalai Lama

Taking care of yourself is one of the biggest factors in staying healthy and maintaining the ideal weight you wish to achieve. Take time to nurture your mind and body. When you take time for yourself, you will have more time and energy to do what needs to be done. This is not being selfish; the intention of loving yourself first will only resonate with people around you. In other words, put your oxygen mask on first and then you can assist others.

One way to do this is to rest and recover by getting the right amount of sleep. Sixty million people in this country suffer from insomnia; it has become an epidemic. A good night's sleep is the cornerstone to good health, and most people need seven to nine hours of sleep each night. In today's fast-paced world, many adults struggle with falling asleep, waking up in the middle of the night, or getting up too early. It's no surprise that these tendencies make you feel sluggish during the day and make it difficult to focus or pay attention due to brain fog. Lack of sleep also affects your waistline, as you will be more apt to succumb to cravings and quick snacks rather than well-planned healthy meals. According to the Institute of Integrative Nutrition, lack of sleep also increases your appetite because two hormones, leptin and ghrelin, stop functioning properly. Leptin's job is to signal to your body that you are full, but lack of sleep suppresses this hormone. At the same time, lack of sleep increases ghrelin, which stimulates appetite. Sleep deprivation also ages your skin, as it leads to puffy eyes, fine lines, and dark circles. The first step in obtaining your optimal weight is to simply make sleeping well a priority. Do yourself a favor and get proper rest.

Sleep health is essential, but nobody's perfect. Maybe you had dinner last night with friends and got home late, or you had good intentions to go to bed early but had trouble falling asleep because your mind was racing. Oh, I've been there! You can try different strategies to figure out what works best for you. Here are ways you can improve your sleep:

1. Creating a space where you feel calm is a key factor in supporting proper sleep hygiene. Keep your bedroom dark at night by using darkening shades or by wearing a sleep mask. Make sure your bedroom is a comfortable temperature. If it's too warm, it could disturb your sleep. Select pillows and bedding that are most comfortable for you.

2. Calm your mind. This means not having any work-related stuff collect in your bedroom, like laundry that needs to be folded or bills that have to be paid. That goes for your laptop also. You know what is going to happen if it is right in front of you... Clear the runway for a good night's sleep.

3. If for some reason you wake up in the middle of the night because something is on your mind, reset your alarm to give yourself a little more time in the morning to sleep. Have a pen and paper on your nightstand to jot down your ideas so you don't worry about forgetting them. Personally, my morning routine takes a backseat to a good night's sleep. Meaning, if I

don't get to exercise or meditate that particular morning, it's okay. A good night's rest is more important to me.

4. It's a good idea to wind down an hour before you go to bed by reading, listening to relaxing music, or meditating. Stay away from violent shows or movies; the content you view can elevate your heart rate, which is what you do not want before bedtime. Personally, I like to take a hot bath in the colder months. I sprinkle lavender essential oils mixed with Epsom salt into my bathwater, and I call this my time to "close out" the day. No matter what happens during the day, I know I will have time to relax at night and clear my mind of chatter from the day.

5. Stick to a sleep schedule. Try to go to bed at the same time every night and wake up at the same time every day. This allows your body to get into a sleep pattern. In addition, staying up late means you are out of sync with nature because of what is called the circadian rhythm. This is basically a twenty-four-hour

clock running in your brain, determining your sleep/wake cycle. This is why it is so important to establish regular sleep habits. Knowing this, it is a good idea to get horizontal – just by simply laying down before 10 p.m. If you stay up later than that, you may notice you get your second wind. Oh, no! Now you'll watch another episode of the latest series you are into or do another load of laundry. Yikes! Before you know it, the clock strikes twelve. When I learned about the importance of sleep, I stopped teasing my husband when I would hear his alarm go off at night to remind him to get to bed. In fact, according to neuroscientist and sleep expert Matthew Walker, setting an alarm in the evening signifying bedtime is equally as important as setting an alarm for waking up. I don't know about you, but I can easily lose track of time.

6.  When working on achieving better sleep, ask yourself: is caffeine making me tired? Although this seems counterintuitive, it can be

true if you don't pay close attention to its effects on your body. I typically enjoy a cup of coffee in the morning – I love the aroma, the taste, and the break it affords me. I have special mugs that I use for each season. Holding a cup of coffee is like holding hands with an old friend, comforting and familiar. Because this is such an enjoyment for me, I decided to continue this feeling by taking a to-go mug with me in the car on my commute to work. One day at the end of the week, I sat down with a friend/colleague before work, just to shoot the breeze and catch up. She is a dear friend who knows me well, so she said, "What's wrong? You look tired, you're not your outgoing self." I began to think about it, and she was right; I wasn't getting the quality sleep I was used to, and I was waking up earlier in the morning than usual. Okay, I got the message – I had to ditch the second cup of coffee and replace it with caffeine-free herbal tea. When it comes to caffeine consumption, whether it is from coffee, tea, or chocolate, there is no right or wrong answer. Some people can have a cappuccino in the evening and sleep just fine, while other people would literally be up all night. Just be conscientious that it is working for you and not against you. Experiencing interrupted sleep patterns could be an indication that you may have to cut back.

As you can see, restful sleep is essential as part of your weight-loss journey. There are simple changes that can be made to remedy poor sleeping habits. I know if I don't get my proper amount of sleep, I'm not on my best game – and my eating habits will get sloppy. Getting the quality of sleep you need is necessary for healing and sustained wellness.

# Chapter 6: Nourish to Flourish

*"You don't have to cook fancy or complicated masterpieces, just food from fresh ingredients."*
– Julia Child

In this chapter, we are going to take a closer look at curbing cravings, making healthy food choices, mindful eating, and meal planning. If you dieted in the past, you have probably experienced the frustration of sticking with a diet while living your normal life. Such diets may require you to replace normal meals with a shake, eat certain foods while omitting others, or count calories or carbs. This takes time, discipline, and a great deal of effort on your part. Then, once you reached a desired weight, *Bam!* You go back to your old eating habits and you know what happens next – the unwanted pounds start to reappear. How crazy does this sound? You shouldn't have to bring your own prepared meal over to your friend's for a dinner party unless of course you have a food allergy or medical condition like celiac disease.

I've seen this happen more than once because someone is trying so hard to stick to their diet. In this book, you are learning about a different approach. You will learn how to listen to your body and make mindful decisions. You also will learn how to acquire a healthy relationship with food.

There are hundreds of diets to choose from in the world, ranging from traditional to the latest fad. Which one really works, and which ones don't? If you follow diets, chances are you will lose weight because you are eating better than you did previously, but really, how long can your body feel restricted without wanting revenge? Sooner or later, your body is going to want to fight back. This is why dieters end up gaining the weight back that they just worked so hard to lose. Personally, I don't diet. Just look at the first three letters of the word: d-i-e. This is not very encouraging, to say the least. I love food too much to sustain a rigid diet, this I know! Eating habits are unique, meaning no one diet works for everyone. One person may be able to handle eating a ribeye steak with a side of mashed potatoes, while another may feel much better eating a burrito bowl loaded with vegetables. You could consider yourself vegan, vegetarian, pescatarian, or flexitarian. There are many variables to consider when discussing taste preferences, such as gender, ethnicity, the particular season it is, and the region in which you live. For example, if you live near the ocean you may include more fish in your diet than if you live in the countryside. In the winter, people prefer heavier foods than they would in the summer. Diets are not one-size-fits-all, but this is what we see when the latest diet trend comes out. There is not much variation among them. Do you see why long-term success is difficult?

## Mindful Eating

For a moment, let's take a look at not what, but how, to eat through mindful eating. Basically, this practice encourages you to pay attention to the food you eat. Mindful eating has little to do with calories, carbohydrates, or fat; it is experienced by slowing down and noticing every bite. It's about exploring the colors and the aroma of your food, savoring each bite, and slowing down and eating without distractions. Mindful eating allows you to follow hunger cues because you are actually listening to your body. You stop when you are near full and you eat when you are hungry. Mindful eating happens when you are sitting at a table instead of grabbing food out of the cupboards and eating on the go. A good conversation during mealtime will interrupt your dinner, extending the duration of a meal. So eating with others is beneficial; it will naturally slow down the eating process because you talk in between bites. By slowing down and eating mindfully, you will find you are satisfied by a much smaller portion than when you are rushed. Mindful eating can't be done while watching television or scrolling through your Instagram feed. Think of what happens when you eat a bucket of popcorn at the movies. You are on autopilot because you are focused on watching the big screen and not on how much popcorn you are eating. Before you know it, the bucket of popcorn is empty. So, before you sit down to a meal, honor your food – take a few deep breaths and be fully present. To cultivate awareness around the eating process, consider doing the following:

- Appreciate the food in front of you. Take a moment and think about how the food is going to fuel your body and give you energy. Take a moment to reflect on the time and effort it took to prepare the meal. Think about the whole journey it took to arrive on your plate, from where it came from to how it was grown.

- Notice if there is an eagerness to begin to eat. Just feel this and don't act on it.

- Are there any feelings that are coming up? Are you excited to eat a meal you made? Or maybe you may feel resistance toward it due to feelings of shame or guilt. Settle in and notice these feelings, then let them pass.

- Begin to activate your senses. What do you see? Notice the vibrant colors and interesting shapes. Is there a sound you hear, like sizzling, associated with the food? What do you smell? Is it a familiar aroma or is it new to you?

- Pick up your utensil. Take slow and deliberate bites. Pay attention to the taste. Savor each bite from the first to the last.

- At the end of the meal, be thankful for the enjoyment you experienced and the nourishment you received.

- Notice how you feel after the meal. Was it just the right amount of food, or perhaps too much or not enough? Use this information to plan your next meal. For example, if you just ate a heavy meal, then balance it off by making your next meal lighter. Perhaps a no-frills salad, a bowl of soup, or scrambled eggs will work.

With practice, you can build awareness and change your relationship with food.

## Meal Planning

Let's face it: there is a lot of delicious food we are susceptible to, and it seems to be everywhere we turn. When we were kids, it wasn't that way. Pizza was basically cheese and pepperoni. We either ate a hamburger with or without cheese. Unless you drove to an ice cream store, your flavor choices were chocolate, strawberry, or vanilla – that was it! Today, there are a zillion choices – just going into a local coffee shop is proof of this. Hot? Cold? A cappuccino? A macchiato? A latte? An espresso? A pour over? Don't get me started on the milk selections...so many options, so little time. Instead of finding yourself confused, winding up eating or drinking something you know isn't going to benefit you, plan what you are going to eat ahead of time.

Planning meals is a proactive way to maintain healthy eating habits and assist in weight loss. This really works for me! Let's say you are going out to dinner with a friend to an Italian restaurant with which you are familiar. You already know they have fresh bread that you can dunk in olive oil and they make the best pasta bolognese, made with homemade pasta. Yum! The diet I offer you isn't a strict set of rules; you can still eat food you enjoy and lose the weight. However, you do need to decide ahead of time what your game plan is so that you don't overeat. For example, you could order the pasta, but make sure to plan ahead of time that you are only going to eat half of the portion and take the rest home. Most restaurants will prepare a generous portion anyway so you are certainly not missing out. In addition, plan on having only a small piece of the crispy bread that you love instead of eating the whole slice. Meals planned for the day, or week, help eliminate spontaneity and uncertainty. If you already know what you are going to eat, you will be less tempted to veer off course, especially when dining out. Also, meal planning will ensure that you feel comfortable when you leave, not stuffed, and you will sleep better too.

So to combat overeating, plan what you are going to eat ahead of time. The same goes for your choice of beverage. As you know, alcoholic beverages can be loaded with sugar and hidden carbohydrates, which will certainly mess with weight loss. Decide whether you are going to have a cocktail with dinner or stick with water. I enjoy a glass of pinot noir or sauvignon blanc with my meal. Wine paired with a meal is delightful – all in moderation. I may have a few glasses of wine a week – anymore and I'm not going to feel good – so I make it part of my plan. How you go about this is up you, so keep in mind you are planning to feel good.

## Home Cooking

Another aspect to consider when eating healthy is eating out versus cooking at home. Restaurants tend to add more salt and sugar to their food to make it taste better, so simply increasing the amount of time you cook at home will benefit your waistline. Home cooking can transform both your physical health and your emotional health. Whether you've blended a smoothie or prepared an entire Thanksgiving dinner, the love you put into it nourishes at an emotional level. When you dine out, the chefs are often stressed. There is a lot of pressure on them at dinner time. Don't get me wrong, I love to go out to eat and enjoy a delicious meal. It's a nice break from the routine, and there are days when I just don't feel like cooking, but think about it – when you prepare a meal at home, you do your best to ensure it is healthy, made with fresh ingredients. I personally sneak kale into meals and my family doesn't even know it. You're not going to get that extra love at a restaurant!

When you prepare a meal at home, you know exactly what is going into your meal. Let's take a closer look. If you prepare a burger at home, you are likely going to choose better-quality beef, with less fat, or use ground turkey. You can add fresh lettuce, tomatoes, onions, or mushrooms, and maybe some avocado. Your meat will sit on a whole-grain bun versus a buttered, flour-enriched one. Replace the fries with string beans, sweet potato wedges, and you have a healthy, delicious home-cooked meal in no time. When you cook at home, you add the ingredients of love and care. Think of how you feel after you have made a nutritious meal for yourself, your family, or a friend. You feel great! Also, cooking is creating – after a while, you can start coming up with your own recipes. It can be fun!

Like the amount of coffee selections you are confronted with at the coffee shop, you have a lot of decisions to make when food shopping. Look down the aisles. They are filled with shelves of numerous brands of bread, and it seems like a new kind of cereal pops up weekly. Where does it end? We are drowning in a plethora of products, and choosing what to purchase nowadays can be an energy-sucking task. Does "Buy one, get one free," or "I had to buy it. It was on sale," sound familiar? Which one is healthier? Food shopping can be draining task. Good nutrition starts with smart choices at the grocery store. Have a list so you know exactly what you need to buy, especially if you are planning your meals for the week. After a while you probably won't even need it. A general rule is to do most of your shopping at the perimeter of the supermarket. This is where you will find the freshest, least-processed foods. Choose a rainbow of fruits and vegetables because they are loaded with vitamins and minerals your body needs. (Yup, Mom was right all along.)

I suggest you choose organic over conventional foods if you can. Organic food is made with fewer pesticides. Though organic food is definitely more expensive, it is money well spent. You can Google the current list of the "Dirty Dozen" and the "Clean Fifteen" to help you make conscious food purchases. The Dirty Dozen refers to twelve crops that feature the highest amounts of pesticide residue. Conversely, the Clean Fifteen refers to crops that have the lowest levels of pesticide contamination. It's also a good idea to buy meat, eggs, and produce from a local farmers' market when available. This food tends to be the freshest because there is little travel time. Local produce ripens naturally, so it retains more nutrients that your body needs.

Eating healthy means cutting down on sugar. There are over sixty names associated with sugar. Some common names are fructose, glucose, maltose, sucrose, and corn syrup. Don't get fooled when reading food labels. It is no secret that sugar is not good for your waistline. Honey, maple syrup, and molasses are better alternatives, but still should be used sparingly.

Carbohydrates get a bad rap in many popular diets. They actually provide us with energy, facilitate healthy digestion, and help support a healthy weight. However, all carbohydrates are not created equal. It's knowing which ones to choose from that makes the difference. You see, there are two categories – simple carbohydrates and complex carbohydrates. Complex carbs are foods like brown rice, quinoa, barley, whole wheat bread, sweet potatoes. These foods provide long-term energy. Simple carbs include white rice, white pasta, white bread, cookies, and granola bars. The fiber has been stripped from these foods, and they can negatively affect your weight. Be conscious of what selections you are making at the grocery store so you are selecting foods to fuel your body. I noticed there are healthier boxed pasta options being sold at the stores these days made with whole or ancient grains and legumes. Over time, you will soon notice that small changes in food selections will have a large impact on your well-being.

## Those Darn Food Cravings

Emotions play a role in producing food cravings. Having a strong desire for a specific food can be a result of stress, fatigue, boredom, or loneliness. In those cases, food won't solve the problem – treating the symptom will. When cravings happen, give yourself some space and examine the cause. The simple act of acknowledging your craving will reduce its power and allow you to detach yourself from it. For instance, if you are noticing that you are eating because you are bored, then perhaps you might want to explore a new hobby like joining a book club or a painting class.

Your body is a well-oiled machine. A lack of vitamins or nutrients can cause you to experience cravings. If you are missing a vitamin or mineral, your body will let you know. Keep in mind that cravings are not always a bad thing. They may be an indication that you are not getting the nourishment your body needs. For example, there are times when I feel like I need a juicy steak, signifying I need more iron. Remember: to practice mindfulness, listen to your body. It knows what it needs.

Take it easy on yourself. Let's face it. We all get cravings. There are going to be times when you just have to go for it. If you don't eat what you desire, you may end up eating more in an attempt to satisfy the craving. Overeating is what you are trying to avoid. To satisfy cravings, be honest with yourself and go for the best-quality foods. If it's chocolate ice cream you want, instead of eating half a dozen chocolate chip cookies and still finding yourself unsatisfied, choose the best-quality chocolate ice cream there is. By doing this, you will feel satisfied. The simple act of indulging once in a while will prevent you from feeling deprived. Similarly, you are going to be in situations that throw you off your game. For instance, I remember once when traveling – which of course will throw anyone off their routine – it was late and I was still hungry. So, when I got to the hotel, I grabbed a bag of potato chips and a bottle of beer at their convenience store. Yes, that was dinner! There are going to be times when you are in situations that interfere with your regular healthy eating habits, but don't fret. Just get back on track the next day. You'll be fine.

## Water

Staying hydrated is important to your overall health and aids in maintaining your ideal weight. The amount of water you should consume varies due to considerations such as weight, gender, activity level, and the climate that you live in. Personally, I aim for eight glasses a day. That may seem like a lot, but you might be consuming more water than you think. You actually get twenty percent of your recommended water intake from eating fruits and vegetables. Foods like cucumbers, lettuce, tomatoes, watermelon, and strawberries contain nearly ninety percent water. Take this into consideration when you are calculating your daily amount. A good habit to get into is drinking a glass of water in the morning right when you wake up. Doing so will help you flush out toxins from your body after a long, restful night's sleep. Although it may sound simple, drinking water will help you maintain your natural weight because it's calorie free, fills you up, and replaces sugary drinks. Personally, I know my skin looks better when I drink my daily amount of water. One of my favorite ways to drink water is with a wedge of lime. To change it up a bit, add fruit or herbs to your glass of water as well.

There comes a day that we realize we are not invincible. We can't indulge in greasy pizza, drink soda, snack on potato chips, and devour a hot-fudge sundae as we did as teenagers. Fogginess, digestion issues, and an expanding waistline are clear signs – to name only a few – that you need to clean up your eating habits. I mentioned you can eat what you want, but you can't get carried away. You'll want to maintain a healthy diet MOST of the time. No need to be perfect. Whether you focus on mindful eating, curbing cravings, or home cooking, the key is to be consistent and create healthy habits. Small steps like this will result in significant changes in how you look and feel over time. Create a plan that will work for you – one that you can stick to and that excites you. You just have to start – that's all. Today, I pay more attention to where my food comes from and I am mindful of how what I ate makes me feel after a meal. I also have learned to make better selections when I go food shopping. I plan out meals because I know that when I am in certain situations, I can easily overeat. Be honest with yourself; do what you can. There is no need to be perfect, just better! Eating nourishing food most of the time will help you look and feel better!

# Chapter 7: Move and Groove

*"Eighty percent of success is showing up."*

– Woody Allen

The word "exercise" can ignite a host of negative feelings. Just the thought of exercise can trigger the mind into thinking, *Ugh, I have to get up early. It's going to be uncomfortable. I've never been successful. Everybody else is in better shape – they are just born with more endurance or have a natural ability to dance and have fun in Zumba class*. Negative chatter can prohibit you from treating yourself to this form of self-care. So, let's take a closer look at the ways exercise can work for you, or how to revamp what you are currently doing so physical activity is a treat!

If you haven't exercised in a while, it's probably a good idea to walk before you run – literally, as you don't want to become overwhelmed. Doing too much too soon can lead to burnout. This is what you are trying to avoid. I know it all too well! For instance, if you use an elliptical machine or treadmill, start with just fifteen minutes a day.

As you continue your exercise routine, you will find that you can easily increase the time on the machine to twenty minutes, then thirty minutes. The same goes with running or walking. Start off small, then gradually increase the distance. The amount of exercise you take part in varies from person to person. Most of all, don't beat yourself up about your current fitness level, your body, or your supposed lack of willpower. It's more important that you are compassionate with yourself, knowing you are taking steps toward well-being.

Ultimately, if you enjoy what you do, you will do more of it. This is the key to a successful exercise routine. Years ago, I participated in highly active fitness classes. At the time, I thought "No pain, no gain." When the class ended, I often ached and felt depleted; I fooled myself into thinking that I "felt good." I dreaded going to the class after a while and stopped going altogether. Does this sound familiar? Even though I was an athlete growing up, I thought that exercise wasn't for me because I was under the impression that it had to be grueling. As I got older, I just wasn't into that kind of workout anymore. Today, I choose only to engage in exercises that I enjoy; yoga, biking, skiing, and walking are activities that I look forward to doing.

A powerful incentive to exercise is to ask a friend to join you. This is a good way to hold one another accountable. For instance, if you plan to go on a brisk walk with friends at seven in the morning, you will more likely show up knowing someone is counting on you. Showing up is half the battle. Also, walking with a friend is a great way to catch up and feel connected. There are two ladies who walk by my house routinely. They are always chatting up a storm when I see them. I've seen them on rainy days, windy days, and wintery days – it doesn't make a difference for them. They have been doing this for years, and I would say they enjoy it!

Certainly, a friend, coworker, or family member can hold you accountable when you need a little encouragement. Another way to make exercise a priority is to pencil in time for it each week. In order to help yourself be successful, simply plan ahead and make time to exercise during the week. Planning in advance will increase the chances that you will stick to a routine. Maybe you like to work out in the morning because you want to begin the day with a clear mind, or possibly a run after work may suit you better to help you relax in the evening. Choose whatever works for you!

Don't be afraid to change your routine or mix it up. Doing the same thing for years may get a little boring. If you're a runner, perhaps you may want to take a yoga or Zumba class to make things interesting. Alternatively, your routine could change with the seasons. Perhaps you like being outside, so you may want to go bike riding twice a week in the summer or go hiking on a nearby trail. Conversely, in the winter, don't let the cold stop you – you could go skiing or snowshoeing. If you belong to a gym, go ahead and try different classes that are offered; you might be surprised to discover something new that you like.

Additionally, don't hesitate to develop your own workout program; the most important thing is that you move – increasing your blood flow, getting your heart rate up, and strengthening your muscles. Take my friend, Malini: she speed walks on the second floor of our building before and some days after work. She does this while listening to her favorite singer. Another friend of mine, Corrine, chooses to march in place on a microfiber rug in the evening in the comfort of her home. No one said your exercise regimen has to be conventional – it all works, my friends! Anything that gets you moving will be beneficial. There is no need to feel like you're training for the Olympics, and both Malini and Corrine are satisfied with the results from their efforts.

You may wonder how regular physical movement will help you. Remember, you are establishing good habits. Newton's first law states that a body in motion stays in motion, and a body at rest stays at rest. With regular movement, you will notice that you will want to continue regular movement throughout your day. To get started, choose movement that agrees with your body. Some people like to go line dancing, and others prefer to swim. Some people love to work in their yard, gardening and raking leaves, which is also a good way to get your body moving. Your choice of physical activity may be a combination of a few different exercises. Remember, whatever works for you may not for someone else, and what you enjoyed doing ten years ago may not suit who you are today. Whatever you choose, do it consistently, and you will see the transformation in no time and will love it! Along with good eating habits, you also want to make exercise a good habit.

You know the role that exercise plays in feeling good because of the fact that while moving you are burning calories and toning muscles. Exercise also does your body good because physical activity acts as a stress reliever. Being active boosts your feel-good endorphins – chemicals in the brain that cope with stress. I know for me, even ten minutes of yoga in the morning calms my mind and allows for a clear perspective before I head off for the day. Besides maintaining your optimal weight, exercise will help you relieve stress, sleep better, and become more focused, and will allow your confidence to grow.

# Chapter 8: Make Your Home a Peaceful Haven

*"We will be more successful in all our endeavors if we can let go of the habit of running all the time, and take little pauses to relax and re-center ourselves. And we'll also have a lot more joy in living."*

– Thich Nhat Hanh

Part of this journey to your natural weight is to enjoy happiness and good health in a warm, welcoming home that inspires you and doesn't drain you. Just as food affects your energy and health, so too does your home environment. You absorb how you feel from your senses. The things you see, hear, smell, and touch affect your physical and emotional health. This is why it is important not to overlook your current living conditions. Home environment varies from person to person and evolves with different stages of your life. While one person may desire an energized space with bright colors and ornate decorations, others may be partial to seeking a calm atmosphere and decorate with soft tones throughout their home. Some people thrive in a minimalist environment while others feel comfortable with a little mess. One person may love living in the city, while another prefers the quiet countryside. As you continue reading, I will share some ideas to enhance your overall home environment no matter your taste preference.

## Improve the Air Quality

Let's face it, many people spend time indoors, so it is important to pay attention to the air quality. You can improve the air quality in your home simply by airing out your house, even during the colder months. Just fifteen minutes will make a difference. Be sure to open your windows during low-traffic times to avoid the exhaust from cars, preferably early in the morning and late in the evening. The first thing I do when I get to work is crack the window open to let the fresh air in. I know people who have improved the air quality in their house by using an air purifier. A natural way to purify air in your home is to add some greenery. Houseplants create not only an ambiance to the home, but convert carbon dioxide into oxygen. Household plants have an overall grounding effect because you bring the outdoors inside when you add them to a room. Why not boost your mood and improve your health by adding some houseplants to your home and workplace?

## Aromatherapy

Ahh! The sense of smell. Whether you want to add a fresh scent or add a little ambiance, candles will do the trick. Your home is your base, so create your peaceful home environment by using candles or oil diffusers to activate your sense of smell. I use soy candles because they are nontoxic, all-natural, and burn longer. When browsing for candles, look for labels that say "one hundred percent soy." I found some to be a blend of soy and paraffin wax. Oil diffusers have become more popular; I often see and smell them at yoga studios, spas, and offices, as well as homes. Incorporating oil diffusers or candles in your home will have a calming effect, contributing to making your home a peaceful retreat.

## Personal Touch

Add a touch of character to your home. Decorate your home with photographs that bring you and your family joy. Snapshots from family vacations, landmark events, or favorite spots in the yard work well. Include candid shots, where family and friends are smiling, laughing, or just acting silly. The idea is that the photographs will bring a smile to your face or will make you chuckle as you walk by them. Hang them on the wall or place them on a side table. I like to purchase paintings from places I've visited because they bring back wonderful memories. I still love the painting my husband and I purchased twenty years ago on our honeymoon in Italy. After all these years, it still brings me joy!

Adding a few throw pillows to a chair or sofa will give your home a warm, inviting feeling. You also can include a classic, cozy throw blanket placed neatly on a sofa in the great room, or added to bedding during the winter months, for an extra touch of warmth. Another nice touch would be to display a favorite book on your coffee table. This book could be used to entertain guests or just provide you with inspiring thoughts as you go about your day.

A fresh bouquet of flowers creates a pleasing look. I have a friend that makes buying fresh flowers her indulgence for the week. You could also create a centerpiece made from fruit. Doing so is cost-efficient and practical. Clementines, limes, and lemons will always provide a natural look for your home. Granny Smith apples, which have a vibrant, green color, will also provide a crisp, clean look in your home. Even better, displaying fruit as home decor only takes seconds to do. Also, with fruit on display, you will most likely grab a healthy snack on your way out the door since it's staring at you, rather than grab an unhealthy snack hidden in the cabinet. It's a win-win!

## Declutter

A clean, comfortable environment reduces stress and therefore is worthwhile to mention as an important factor in weight reduction. Imagine walking into a house after a long day at work where the laundry is in piles in the family room, kitchen countertops are full of papers and dirty dishes, and your office space is transformed into a playroom. Mentally, you are all over the place, which makes it harder to focus. Where do you go to relax after a long, stressful day? At this point you are too tired to think about creating a healthy meal – you just want to get your family fed. Just as you fill your body with healthy foods and engage in physical movement, it's important to create a home that lights you up.

A component of creating a healthy home is letting go of items that no longer have value or bring you happiness. If you're already a minimalist, you've got this already. Whether you are aware or not, there is a direct correlation between household clutter and personal health. Some are obvious ways clutter can be an obstacle, such as not being able to find your eyeglasses or cell phone, and some are not so obvious, like holding on to items that you don't use anymore, such as outdated television remote controls. Disordered things can cause behaviors such as indecisiveness and make you feel uneasy. You simply cannot make your best choices in a disorganized home. It is hard to feel calm when items are scattered around the house. This disorder prohibits you from seeing clearly and goes against a peaceful mind. In his book *Lose the Clutter, Lose the Weight,* Peter Walsh writes, "Women whose homes were more stressful – based partly on their home's clutter levels – had a pattern of changes in their cortisol levels that showed more chronic stress." Stress  potentially causes a host of diseases in the body, one of which is weight gain. Today we have more stuff than ever, and having an excessive amount of stuff has been linked to stress and anxiety, which can be emotionally draining. We live in an era where more stores than ever have well-stocked shelves, not like when I was growing up. I don't remember having a lot of stuff or feeling like we needed more. We seemed perfectly content going without it.

The piles of clutter aren't only in your way, but they also give energy to the stuff that weighs your life down. Remember, the way you do one thing is the way you do everything. Having a lot of belongings can contribute to overeating simply through the chronic thought that you feel like you need more. Grabbing for snacks when you aren't really hungry is a common response to feeling overloaded.

There are a number of reasons we hold on to stuff. Sometimes we think we might need it "someday." Holding on to something because we think we might need it in the future is rubbish. As a matter of fact, that's probably where the outdated item belongs – in the rubbish. We also hold on to items because we get caught in the past or, simply, we don't know what to do with them. Clearing out rooms actually clears out your mind. The outer world reflects your inner world. Does any of this sound familiar?

Another reason clutter accumulates is from fear of making a mistake. People will think, *Oops, I shouldn't have thrown away my daughter's childhood books*. I have a solution that will help you. Have each of your children get one storage container and have them place childhood memories inside. Keep only what fits in the container. When they are adults and go off on their own, they take their storage container with them. This system will help you manage how much space you are going to allocate for family memoirs.

Lastly, we hold on to things because we get stuck in the past. However, items that were functional a decade ago may not necessarily be so functional today. Get rid of what no longer serves you. Yes, that means your collection of CDs you have in a box in the basement. I'm sure your local library would love them. Again, small steps will make a big difference. Start with one shelf, and then move on to a closet, followed by a whole room. In no time, you will see and feel the difference.

When simplifying, there are several options. For example, you can bring your items to a consignment shop to be sold, or you may enjoy selling your items yourself on websites like eBay or Craigslist. You could also have a yard sale, either by yourself or by pairing up with a neighbor. This way, you declutter and make some money. Alternately, you could donate to organizations, such as

The Salvation Army or Goodwill. I've put unwanted items at the end of my driveway and placed a sign on them that reads, "Free, take me." Within two days, they are gone. Reducing clutter may be as easy as giving your old patio furniture set away to someone just starting out. Why does this simple act feel so good? You're helping someone else out. That's why.

One caveat to keep in mind, however: having an orderly, clean teenager's room. When I walk into my daughter's room, I scan for any traces of food that could potentially turn into a science experiment. Instead of getting upset, I collect it, close the door, and walk away. Of course, teenagers need their own private space. When the moon and sun are properly aligned, they will clean their rooms and throw away what they don't need; until then, they are pretty content and probably know where everything is.

You want to enter a warm, welcoming home so that you are able to live in the present moment. This means surrounding yourself with items you cherish and that have meaning for you and your family. Items from the past include old cell phones, old clothes, old makeup, outdated books, etc. Do you really need your grandmother's china set that you haven't used in twenty years sitting in your basement? Time to let it go!

I want to be clear that by no means should your goal be making your house perfect. No need to go crazy here. Just reflect on where you are in the area of home environment to ensure it is aligned to your needs. Remember: progress, not perfection. I actually like it when I step on my dog's squeaky toys in the middle of the kitchen floor. It makes me smile every time. Keeping a tidy house should not steal from you the joy of spending quiet time by yourself or quality time with others. Rather, these are simple steps you can take to live in a relaxed environment to bring you comfort and ease. Even small changes can bring about a transformation.

## Good Vibes Only

What is a vibe and what is its place in your home? You can't see a vibe and you can't buy it, but you sure can feel it. A vibe is a warm, fuzzy feeling you get from a person, place, or situation. You feel welcomed, happy, and grounded from good vibes creating good moods. Just as I wrote this chapter, my husband, Michael, walked into the house and said that he was watching a beautiful yellow bird – a warbler – fly onto the patio. Then he spotted two wrens frolicking under the patio table. As if rehearsed, the warbler flew away and a dove landed on the roof of our home. This perfect bird musical lasted for roughly two minutes. Yeah, I'm convinced our backyard has good vibes. To get my point across, I share this experience with you. Life is happening all around us; we just have to clear the way to be able to notice it. Although I don't have the power to orchestrate the previous bird scene, I can certainly fashion the space to allow it to happen. In the same way the Iowa farmer played by Kevin Costner in the 1989 movie *Field of Dreams* built a baseball diamond on his land as a result of hearing a mysterious voice say, "If you build it, they will come," you can set up a positive space for good vibes to enter your home. Costner's character experienced the ghosts of great players emerge from the crops to play baseball, and you can create the space for greatness as well. You are so worth it!

Living a healthy life includes creating a comfortable environment. Your home, whether it's an apartment, condo, or house, can either inspire or drain you. Make your home a relaxing place to come back to at the end of the day – make your home a sanctuary. Reflect on your current situation: how does your home make you feel? How is your ideal home environment different than your current home? What small changes can you make to appeal to your senses? My friends, this is part of healthy living and sustained weight loss.

# Chapter 9: Money Matters

*"Too many people spend money they have not earned to buy things they don't want to impress people they do not like."*

– Will Smith

Yes, a chapter on finances definitely needs to be included in this book because money, whether you have an abundance of it or not, will have an effect on your overall well-being. It is one of the biggest causes of stress. Finances include your income, savings, investments, and spending. The idea is to have a healthy relationship with money in order to cultivate stability and security for you and your family. Overall, you want to be in a position of confidence, knowing how much to spend and save. It is important to be responsible with your finances so you can use your money and plan for your future with ease.

Our emotions such as fear, blame, envy, insecurity, and anger can be linked to money. I know I've gone shopping for clothes I didn't need when I felt like I needed a boost, then felt ashamed because I spent too much. Our emotions can get the best of us; it seems like everyone is trying to keep up with the latest gadgets, cars, vacations, and houses. You go out of your way to get the best deal. You want to fit in and not feel like you lack anything or have less than someone else. Additionally, you may harbor a belief that all your problems are caused by a lack of money. You may think you were not allotted your fair share in a divorce or inheritance. You might also have beliefs from childhood that there will always be an inadequate amount of money, or you may simply feel that there is not enough to go around. To curb these feelings toward money, consider the following steps:

1. Become aware of your emotions. Take time to examine your feelings. What feelings are surfacing? For example, not having enough money to buy what you want, or feeling guilty that you haven't been charitable.

2. Create a positive money mindset. Money allows you to put food on the table and have a roof over your head. You either feel abundance and in control, or feel scarcity, as if money controls you. In order to have an abundance of money, you have to first foster a positive mindset. There is plenty to go around. You have to tease out any limiting beliefs you have about money.

Throughout this book, you hear that you can change your old thought patterns and create new ones, and your thoughts around money are no different.

3. Lastly, you need to take action. You will need to follow a budget and take responsibility for your money. Begin to take control of your money so that you will make choices that are aligned to your goals.

## Healthy Spending

Let's dive into budgeting. According to Manisha Thakor, founder of MoneyZen, in an ideal world there is a general rule to what she calls "healthy spending." She recommends using the "50-30-20" budgeting rule. These numbers refer to the percentage of how you should allocate your income after taxes. It goes like this: *fifty percent* of your take-home income should go toward the items you need to pay for, such as housing, transportation, food, mandatory debt paydown, and childcare. *Thirty percent* of your income should be allocated for activities and purchases you want, like travel, concerts, and going out to eat. The last *twenty percent* of your income goes toward savings. The savings can be broken down into three components: emergency fund, intermediate-term goals (education, car, wedding), and retirement. Keep in mind that this is a general rule. If you are only able to save five percent, that's a start. At the end of the day it's about progress, not perfection. It's worthwhile to do a check-in to see how close your finances are compared to the "50-30-20" budget rule. The idea is to try to keep your finances in balance so you can pay your bills, save your money, have fun, and reduce your stress.

Today, there are many online solutions at your fingertips that you can use to balance your finances, such as Mint or Quicken. These apps can easily analyze your monthly spending to calculate how close your spending is to the "50-30-20" rule. My husband and I go over our budget together yearly to see if we are balancing our income. This way, we can set goals for upcoming projects for the house, vacations, and paying for college.

# Taking Responsibility for Your Money

Taking control of your finances includes taking steps to become debt-free. First, to do this, you need to pay down your credit card debt. If you have more than one credit card balance, consider consolidation to reduce or eliminate the interest rate applied to the balance to a card with a lower interest rate. Not only do late payments increase the amount of interest that needs to be paid, but they also take a toll on your credit score. Lenders use credit scores to determine who qualifies for a loan, at what rate, and at what credit limits. Paying your bills on time and paying the balance are essential steps toward taking control of your finances. Additionally, along with chipping away at your credit card debt, your next focus should be on paying off your mortgage. Each time you pay more than your monthly payment, the money is applied to your principal balance. If done consistently, the result is a staggering savings on your mortgage interest by reducing the number of years on the loan.

Another tip is to look closely at your monthly credit card statement and examine if there are any reoccurring expenses that you no longer use. You may find you no longer need the movie subscription or find a less expensive option. When payments are automatic, they are often forgotten.

Next, establish an emergency fund so you will be prepared to handle whatever financial situation life throws at you. Give yourself this peace of mind and set a goal to plan for the future. How much money should be in your emergency fund? This varies depending on your monthly costs, dependents, income, and lifestyle. The general rule is to put away three to six months' worth of expenses. Whatever the amount is, putting money away for an emergency will free you from unnecessary stress, knowing you are prepared to deal with an unexpected event.

Feel confident in your financial future by investing as much as you can in a retirement fund – the reason being that the money is tax deferred. For example, if you are in a 24% tax bracket, that means for every $1.00 you are saving toward retirement, you actually are saving $1.24. You'll be surprised how fast this money grows.

Look at the way you spend money, and ask yourself, "Do I really need it?" For instance, look at the money you could save on your everyday expenditures, such as if you brewed your own coffee instead of purchasing a $4 cup. Consider the money you could save if you packed your own lunch for work instead of eating out. It all adds up. Saving $30 a week on these expenditures totals $120 in savings each month. Over a year, you would save $1,440.

Now, if you are in the position that you have financial security, you are not off the hook. You still have to pay attention. I remember watching an interview with

Michael Jordan's mother on television. As you well know, Michael Jordan is considered one of the great NBA players of all time and has made millions of dollars. I remember his mother's words of wisdom. She said, "No matter how much money you make, you still need a budget." You can't be reckless with your money. You still have to have a plan in place. You have to consider what charitable organizations you going to support. Donors should align the cause with their own passions and interests. You'll have to do the research. Think about how you can be a positive influence on the world.

Money does matter when it comes to your health. Without even knowing it, a financial burden causes a host of health issues. Worrying, lack of clarity, and uncertainty create upheaval for your whole family. This is definitely a touchy subject, but it is important for couples to be open and on the same page when it comes to finances. Whatever your arrangement is, have a plan and stick with it, because sticking to a budget will empower you to plan for your future so that you can do more of the things you enjoy!

# Chapter 10: Build Your Tribe

*"You yourself, as much as anybody in the entire universe, deserves your love and affection."*

– Buddha

As humans, we have a deep desire to connect and be with one another. Social interaction gives us a chance to exchange ideas and lend support. Not only are social connections pleasurable, but they are also as important to our health as adequate sleep, good eating habits, and a proper exercise routine. Humans are social beings. Social networking has made it easier to connect with people from all over the world. We can easily get in touch with like-minded people. Although our contacts may be vast, people still need physical contact. Human beings need face-to-face interaction. We need to be able to shake hands, have eye contact, and engage in hugs and kisses. A sense of belonging is a basic psychological need for survival. According to Dan Buettner, who studies areas in the world where people live the longest, healthiest lives, people who have social support are happier, live longer, and have fewer health problems.

## Love Thyself

First, let's examine your relationship with yourself. This is your most important relationship, yet it can be so easily overlooked. Are you a perfectionist? Do you feel like your best isn't good enough? Do you have a tendency to procrastinate or avoid challenges in fear of getting it wrong? Striving for perfection means you're setting yourself up for failure because it demands unattainable outcomes. Perfectionism is often confused with striving for excellence, which is altogether different. Aiming for excellence is a direction, not an endpoint. It's about focusing on your achievements – acknowledging how far you've come. Having this mindset will only energize you and build your self-esteem. Perfectionism, on the other hand, causes anxiety and is draining because you zero in on what you haven't done. Striving for excellence is pursuing what matters to you instead of honing in on what others will think of you. This is why, when going through a transformation such as weight loss, it is important to remember you are doing this to feel your best so that you shine from within, not to please others with how you look. Be compassionate with yourself and embrace what is "going well," and have fun with the process!

Another step to loving yourself is to practice forgiveness. This includes forgiving yourself as well as others. I often felt guilty about working full time when my daughter was young. Yes, I suffered from "mommy guilt." I remember the day my daughter begged me to be a chaperone for her class on her fourth-grade field trip to Plymouth Rock. At that time, I felt I couldn't miss work so I said, "No." Of course, it ended up being a beautiful November day, much warmer than usual for that time of the year. It seemed as though all the other parents played hooky from work that day to accompany their child. Ugh! I replayed that bad decision over and over in my head for years. Why? I felt guilty! At that time, it was my decision. Although she was disappointed, my daughter survived and turned out just fine. I was able to join her on future field trips. How does replaying that incident serve me now? These feelings just drain you and actually block you from staying in the present moment – the place where you experience joy. Come to the understanding that feelings of guilt are all part of your journey. We live, we learn, we grow, we get better. If a feeling of guilt arises, or any other negative feeling for that matter, simply acknowledge it, let it pass, be compassionate, and forgive yourself. Don't try to suppress these negative emotions or make them linger. You can't alter the past no matter how many times you recapitulate the situation in your head. However, you CAN choose to change the story you've been telling yourself. Instead of feeling frozen in guilt for not being present, I think, *Wow, my daughter is growing up to be an independent lady*. Also, the guilt I was feeling made me realize I had to let go of my ego and prioritize what is truly important in my life – family. I acknowledged my feelings, rewrote my story, and came out better. If I continued harboring thoughts of guilt or shame, it would just rob me of what is happening in the present moment.

We also have to let go and forgive others. At some point in our adult lives, everyone has experienced episodes of betrayal, disappointment, abandonment, deceit, manipulation, and trauma. This doesn't mean you have to live with these experiences, allowing them to take control over you. Those unfortunate experiences will have a grasp on you until you forgive whoever wronged you in the past. This is not to say you condone what happened; it's just about recognizing negative events so you can heal from them. During these times, you build your inner strength and evolve. When you forgive someone, you do so for yourself, not the other person. Forgiveness is more powerful than you think. Through forgiveness, you move forward and release yourself from the past so you can get back into the present moment.

Do yourself a big favor and don't compare yourselves to others – not to your friends, family, neighbors, or colleagues. Remember, you are who you are supposed to be and nobody else. Think about it: why should living your life like someone else make you happy? We all are on our own life journey. We learn from our own experiences and have our own dreams. These days, it is so easy to look at social media and feel as if you are not enough, especially when everyone around you seems to be enjoying lavish vacations and doing exciting activities when you're not. Friends, what you see on social media is not the whole story, just a fraction of it. You're not seeing the whole picture. You can't compare yourself to a fraction of a person. In other words, you have to dance to the beat of your own drum. We are all unique; out of a trillion snowflakes, no two are alike, and neither are humans. Sometimes we feel ahead on our path and other times we feel like we are trailing behind. You just might not be where you desire to be, YET, but be patient knowing you are on your way. Don't let go of your dreams; it is quite normal to experience doubts when going through a transformation. When these uneasy feelings arise, remember to stay focused and continue forward on your weight-loss journey.

## Setting Boundaries

How do you recognize people with whom you need to establish boundaries? Well, you often feel depleted, or like you are walking on eggshells because you don't want to say the wrong thing. That's how. These unhealthy relationships can have physical implications as well. For example, I had an acquaintance once that I bumped into while shopping. I wanted to catch up, but for her, this was an opportunity to dump her "crap" on me. She went on and on so much so that I developed a pain in my chest that continued into the next day. Has this ever happened to you? Being an energy-sensitive person, I absorbed her negative energy like a sponge. These people most likely are not listening to your advice; they are just dumping their problems on you, without regard to what it is doing to your emotional state. While these individuals might not necessarily be bad people, they are prohibiting you from becoming your best self by being energy suckers. In fact, they might not even know the negative impact they have on you. Here's some Psychology 101 for you: a friendship occurs when both people give and take – a relationship of equals. In other words, there is listening and speaking from both parties involved. In fact, this wisdom is actually something I do remember learning from one of the first psychology classes I took in college. On the other hand, good friends are seeking your advice and needing your guidance because they wish to get past the issue. Good friends trust each other and care for one another. Yes, we all need a shoulder to cry on once in a while, especially if we are going through a traumatic event. Friends provide one another comfort. Let's face it: we all need to vent our frustrations from time to time. It's healthier to let off some steam than it is to hold your emotions inside. I know it makes me feel better because it reduces emotional intensity. Ideally, you want to get to the point where you can SOLVE the issue. Rather, toxic people look for an audience to listen to their tales of woe. They want you to feel bad with them and don't have any intention to take action toward fixing the problem. Victims aren't listening! You shouldn't have to lower your energy to help someone.

You need to be proactive in maintaining healthy relationships. When setting boundaries, be straightforward. Tell whatever energy drainers you are dealing with that it is not okay to be treated the way they treat you. You can also let them know what kind of effect the behavior has on you. Don't let them suck you into listening to their low-energy stories. The more you listen, the more they will talk. So, a strategy to use when you feel this occurring is to stop them in their tracks. First, recognize how they feel, then change the subject or exit the conversation altogether. A solution to my previous encounter with my acquaintance might go like this: "Hey, sounds like you're going through a rough time right now. I'm sure you will figure it out." Leave it at that! Don't get sucked into the low-energy conversation. Finally, know when to limit your time with someone. When people's dramatic patterns repeat over and over again, this behavior is a lifestyle and you find yourself and others always running to the rescue. Your time and who you spend it with is your choice!

In order to be your best, it's important to recognize that toxic relationships cause stress with repeated encounters. Stress takes a toll on your body and can interfere with you sustaining your optimal weight. You don't need to feel that you owe anyone anything. It's not your job to fix other people's problems. They must do this for themselves. Instead, focus your energy on the positive people in your life. The more you radiate positive thoughts, words, and actions, the more you will attract people into your life who do the same.

## Support System

Some people are in your life forever. Others swing in and out of your life for a "season," as they should. Your time together begins and ends. For example, I had a wonderful friend in graduate school named Erica. We met while student teaching together at the same school and became fast friends. We spent a lot of time together working, studying, and socializing – playing endless games of Pictionary on Friday nights with friends. I felt like she was more of a sister to me than a friend. Soon after we graduated, we lost touch. Some friendships are like that; they have expiration dates, which is okay. Of course, I missed Erica, but we both needed to move on. We each needed mutual support and company at that particular time and place to achieve the same goal. People will come in and out of your life at the right time. Like Erica, they were not meant to stay forever. This is all part of your journey.

In high school, we spend years trying to fit in. Our clothes, hangouts, and activities are influenced by our peers. There are also different herds in school – the athletes, artists, and chess club kids. As adults, we are no longer surrounded with people of our same age or who grew up in the same town. Our contacts broaden, giving us more freedom to become who we are. Yes, you will share commonalities with people, like work, living in the same neighborhood, or practicing the same workout routine, but you bring more diversity to the table. Your connection with people will be based more on how you make them feel and less on geography.

We all are drawn to people who like to have fun and laugh, so make these individuals part of your tribe – the people you can count on, who encourage you, and with whom you like spending time. If you are funny, share your sense of humor; however, make sure your laughter is not at the expense of others. Laugh with, not at, people. Laughter is a great way to draw people into your life. Personally, there is no better way to lighten your life than to experience a good, spontaneous, communal belly laugh – one that makes you cry and your stomach ache. Whoever said "Laughter is the best medicine" was right. Laughter can instantly diffuse a tense moment, and has healing properties; just as exercise does. Laughter also stimulates the heart and lungs and triggers the release of endorphins that help you feel more relaxed, both physically and emotionally.

Just about every day, my colleagues and I gather for lunch. No matter what kind of a morning we have, we come together for half an hour of good conversation and laughter while we share ideas and eat, recharging our minds. Our conversations include a variety of topics – movies, concerts, sports, and memories from childhood. We have mutual respect for one another, so the conversation starts off with a spontaneous thought that develops into an intriguing conversation. Not only does our gathering together fulfill a need for social connection, we also offer each other advice and support.

What kind of people do you connect with? Are they supportive, nourishing? Having this sense of connection with others can be a catalyst for joy. You have begun the journey to lose weight, so frequently spend time with people who support you and your goals. Surrounding yourself with supportive people, your tribe, will only encourage you to keep going. Your tribe could be a lunch group or a single friend like Erica. Both serve the same purpose. I sometimes catch myself watching bicyclists riding in a group on the side of the road. I've always been fascinated by how they ride in harmony; each stride appears equally timed. Bicyclists ride in one straight line in unison, fully focused on the task. The synergy between them allows them to ride longer and faster than if they were riding separately.

Connecting with people gives you a great sense of fulfillment – especially during times of personal growth. Being part of a community and having strong social relations have positive psychological effects. Take a moment to check in with yourself and determine if you need to find a tribe or evolve your current tribe so that it is aligned with your weight-loss goals. Surrounding yourself with people who support you on your weight-loss journey will only energize you and propel you forward.

# Chapter 11: Do What You Love, Love What You Do

*"I never did a day's work in my life. It was all fun."*

– Thomas Edison

Your career will have a significant effect on your weight-loss journey because it is such a huge part of your daily life. More than half of our waking hours are spent working at our jobs. What you do for a living will either enhance your life or take away from your health and vitality. Doing the work you love will supercharge you, bring you joy, and keep you motivated. On the other hand, an unfulfilling job can cause stress, boredom, and sickness, which can disrupt your weight-loss journey. I find far too many times people are working to reach the goal of "retirement." What! Retirement isn't a goal, rather it is a transition – I know many people who continue to work or volunteer. So, you have a choice to either find the work you love or find a way to love the work you do.

You don't necessarily have to change careers altogether if you are not content with your current job. You may just have to make some changes within your current position. Let's take a look at Terry, for example. She worked as a registered nurse during the night in a hospital. She has done this for six years. Just this past year she seemed to struggle with more colds than usual and unforeseen weight gain. She loved her career but was starting to feel resentful about working at night. She wanted to have a schedule more in sync with her boyfriend's so they could spend more quality time together. After careful reflection, she decided she needed to switch to the day shift. She had to wait a few months for the right position to open up. By remaining patient and focused, she now works the day shift, which suits her current needs better. Even though the hospital is busier during the day, she feels more at ease because she is sleeping better and doesn't feel "out of the loop" with her loved ones. Like Terry, reevaluate your current job. If you are not satisfied, you may just need to make an adjustment in order to love your work again.

Some things to think about would be: What do you want your working environment to look like? How will you interact with your colleagues? Do you want to work remotely? Do you want a flexible schedule? Do you need benefits? Is there room for growth? I remember when my job as a math coach was being consolidated and I had to look for another position within the school department. I narrowed my search down to four criteria. I wanted to teach in an air-conditioned building. I wanted to teach with like-minded people. I wanted a shorter commute than I currently had. I wanted to be an intermediate elementary grade teacher. This is what I wanted, and this is what I received. Be clear with your goals.

Maybe you just need a boost by making your workspace a more pleasant working environment. You can do this by adding plants or personal photos to your space. Use a favorite pen or decorative sticky notes. I recently added an essential oil diffuser to my workspace to promote a calming, welcoming atmosphere.

Keep your eye out for new opportunities to learn. Many companies offer professional development workshops, conferences, classes, and webinars. Learning new skills can give you a fresh outlook and keep you engaged. It can sharpen your knowledge, especially if you are feeling rusty. Maybe a colleague has a solution you were looking for. We can certainly learn a lot from each other. There is always room to fine-tune your craft.

Your satisfaction with your career can often ebb and flow throughout the year. For instance, if you work in retail, you will undeniably face more pressure during the holiday season. The same goes if you are an accountant. You're going to feel overworked and out of balance during tax season. We know life will not be smooth sailing all the time. Know that "this, too, shall pass," a famous quote repeated by Eckhart Tolle. Yes, you will be challenged, but it will not last forever. The only thing that is certain is change. Ups and downs come with any lifelong quest, even in a job you love. You just have to take a deep breath and keep calm and ride the wave to shore.

If you need a super-refresher from your current job, then don't hesitate to take a vacation. We all need a break in our normal routine. Whether getting away for a long weekend or spending a week on an idyllic Caribbean island vacation, both serve the same purpose. The word "vacation" comes from the Latin word "vacare," meaning "to be empty, be free." What does that tell you? The time off is time well spent recharging your batteries. When you have a break, participate in leisurely activities, refrain from looking at your e-mails, and limit your time on social media. Both your mind and body need a rest. Another option is to take part in a staycation. Use your time to stroll through a local park or visit a museum. Dive into a backyard pool or go boogie boarding at the beach. Makes plans for lunch dates with friends and family. Clearly, staycations can be just as purposeful as a break spent far from home. We can be so overloaded at times. So, in order to curtail burnout, you need to recalibrate by stepping away. The results are well worth it.

You don't have to stay in the same job or field; we definitely have more career freedom now to make a change than we did years ago. If you no longer feel satisfied or enriched from your work because it is no longer aligned with your values, goals, or lifestyle, then you need to search for what will bring you joy, as it will take a toll on your overall health. What you found fulfilling twenty years ago may not suit you today. Be patient – finding a new career may not happen instantly. You may have to try a few positions before you settle in.

Just know how important it is to do what you love, as it will affect your well-being and ideal weight.

I came to realize I don't have to be one or the other. What fits in my world is being an elementary school teacher and a health coach. This definitely involves time management. I realize in order to do both I can't get involved with every after-school activity, so I plan out ahead of time what I am able to do throughout the year. I also schedule a set time to write and coach. This is where I am now; this is what I enjoy.

Finding how you love to spend your time doesn't necessarily mean finding it through a career. You may find what thrills you is your hobby. I recently met a photographer named Bob. His passion is to take photographs of railroad trains. Bob started doing this after he retired. He has been up and down the East Coast looking to capture the perfect snapshot of a locomotive. He said he always loved the aesthetics of trains. I asked him what he does with his photographs – he replied, "I frame them and hang them around my house." How you know you are on the right track doing what you love – it puts a smile on your face and fully engages you. This was evident as I listened to Bob's story. I've talked about exercising your body, but remember, you also have to exercise the mind – via career or hobby.

There is a long life to live. When I was a student at the Institute of Integrated Nutrition, I learned that in general, people now live longer. In the 1800s, the average life expectancy in the United States was thirty-five. In the 1900s, the life expectancy was only forty-seven years old. Today, average life expectancy is seventy-eight years old. Clearly, there has been a significant increase; it nearly doubled in one hundred years. I am here to tell you that you have a long life to live. This really resonated with me. I realized I need to design my life the way I wanted to live and not just let inertia take hold of the steering wheel. Check in with this area of your life. Notice what lights you up. Are you doing what you love? Are you spending time with people who energize you? Are you getting paid fairly? Are you in a job that allows for creativity and growth? You have to plan today for the life you want tomorrow. It is not going to happen all by itself. As we see a steady trend in an increase in life expectancy, be wise and spend your time doing what brings you joy.

# Chapter 12: Practice Gratitude with Attitude

*"Calm mind brings inner strength and self-confidence, so that's very important for good health."*

– Dalai Lama

## Spirituality

Whatever "spirit" means to you, just knowing that there is a broader purpose for your existence is vital for your well-being. Being spiritual fosters a sense of comfort, hope, love, and relaxation. Spiritual practice looks different for everybody; it could be attending weekly service, engaging in daily prayer, meditating, practicing yoga, or simply taking a walk outdoors and communing with nature. Fostering spirituality very well may be a combination of all of those activities. Your personal identification with spirituality may alter throughout your life. Whatever resonates with you, having a sense of spirituality is an important part of the weight-loss journey.

Being spiritual is believing you are part of something bigger than yourself. You know you are connected to a higher being; Source, Universe, God, Spirit, inner guidance, or whatever term you use. You feel guided and are open to receiving messages from Spirit – confirming that you are on the right course. Writing this book has been an intricate part of my own transformation. During this process, I had to dig deep, question, reflect, and be vulnerable. When you're stirring up these feelings, questions and doubt arise. *Could I really make a difference with this book? It is so easy not to do it and remain stagnant. I am quite comfortable where I am, I really don't need to do this.* Here is what I believe was the Universe's response to my ambivalence. Just as I was doubting myself, two ladies rang my doorbell. *Hmm...* They said they were from the Jehovah's Witnesses Hall in town. *No big deal, they've come to the house before.* Apparently, that morning they were going door to door to speak with neighbors. They were harmless so I listened to what they had to say even though I had no intention of joining the group. Interestingly, the reason I was home at all to answer the doorbell was because I was meeting my talented cabinet maker, Joey, at my house at 10:30 so he could complete some small jobs that needed to be finished. Our original meeting time was at 11 a.m., but Joey called me to tell me he was running early – not typically the words you hear. Knowing this, I made sure I was home at 10:30 so as not to keep him waiting. Gayle, the woman at my door, began to read scripture – Matthew 6:9, 10, "Through his Kingdom, Jehovah will soon end the suffering of each individual." I thought to myself: *If you are not feeling your best, then you are suffering.* This wasn't only a reading; it was divine intervention telling me I had a job to do. *Okay, I got the message!* My navigation was set back on track. Now, this vignette gets even better! What time do you think I opened my computer to write this chapter? 1:11 p.m., of course. For those of you who are not familiar, 111 is an "angel number." Angel numbers are sequences of numbers, like 111, that carry divine guidance. Seeing 111 is telling you that whatever you are doing, it is meant to be. It is telling you that you are on the right path. The Universe communicates to you how it can – through people, nature (birds, flowers, wind, sunshine, songs, etc.), and numbers. This did not happen just by chance. Remember, you are not in it alone. Are you noticing any of these signs? How is the Universe speaking to you and supporting your transformation? All you have to do is believe. Before, I would have walked past – no, ran right by – the signs that unfolded in front of me. I realize now that there are no coincidences, only synchronicity. You just have to recognize it!

## Meditation

Meditation has been around for thousands of years, and it has become an increasingly popular tool used to overcome stress and increase well-being. Meditation is a practice of aligning your mind and spirit. By meditating, your mind becomes still, which brings about clarity and awareness. Studies show that the regular practice of meditation delivers consistent, positive effects on our physical and mental well-being. The positive effects include decreasing stress and anxiety, increasing energy, fostering creativity, increasing problem-solving skills, and improving sleep. Let me remind you that proper sleep and stress reduction are essential parts of sustained weight loss.

Through meditation, we are able to step away from the clutter or noise in life brought about by juggling aspects of our lives such as our finances, career, health, and relationships. We become like robots, mindlessly going from one activity to another. Meditation trains our brains to slow down. As you can see, meditating is a valuable investment in well-being. This is why it has become part of my morning routine.

There are different types of meditation. I would like to mention two approaches that I find helpful. First, you can meditate simply by focusing on the breath. An example of mindful breathing meditation is called "square breathing." It includes four steps, each done to the count of four. Easy to remember. First, find a comfortable posture either sitting, lying down, or standing. Soften or close your eyes. Now, focus your attention on your breathing. Continue doing this as you inhale and exhale. Begin to inhale through your nose as you count to four. Feel your lungs expanding like a balloon. Then, hold your breath for four counts. Next, exhale through your mouth for four counts. Lastly, hold the exhale for four seconds. Repeat this process for several rounds. You will immediately feel a calming sensation. I've used these breathing techniques when I am on the go. This is a great tool to use when stuck in traffic (keep your eyes open for this one), during moments of tension at your workplace, or when you're struggling to get through a hectic day. It really does work!

Another form of meditation is guided meditation. If you're like me and your mind has a tendency to wander, you may find meditating with guidance will help you stay in the present moment. No need to worry – if thoughts do arise, know that it's normal and part of the process. Let them flow in and out. This meditation can be guided by a teacher, at a studio, or through audio or video. It can be done alone or in a group setting. Either way, your guide will instruct you to relax specific muscles and will lead you through visualizations or ask you to repeat a specific mantra. There are tons of videos online to choose from. The positive effects of meditation occur even when meditating for only five minutes a day. However, for optimal results, a daily meditation practice of twenty minutes or longer yields the best results.

If meditation is not for you, then just getting outside can do you a world of good. Being in nature can make you feel grounded and quiet the chatter in your mind much like meditation does. So, take a walk on the beach and listen to the waves crash. Go on a hike. Take a walk around the block. Sit outside and watch the sun set in the distance as it says goodbye to another day. Just being outside in nature will clear your mind and boost your mood for sure.

## Gratitude

Every sunrise begins a brand-new day, allowing you to start fresh. I see this principle when I awake each morning after my alarm goes off and I am greeted by my dog, Bella. She is a nine-pound Shih Tzu, Maltese, and King Charles mix. Yes, she is very cute! As soon as she notices I'm awake, Bella instantly walks over to greet me, wagging her tail and rubbing her wet nose against my cheek. She even sometimes gives me kisses. Bella is bursting with excitement, simply because it's a brand-new day. If she could talk in those moments, she would probably say, "Good morning, so happy to see you." Bella reminds me to be thankful for another day. You begin your journey to a healthy life anew each morning. It doesn't matter what happened yesterday, just be thankful for today!

The way to change how you feel when you're in a funk is to simply change your perspective. The circumstances don't change, but once your attitude changes you will begin to see solutions to your problems. Opportunities appear that may have been overlooked. It's your choice. You can either be grateful for what you have or be stuck in limiting beliefs about what you don't have. If the day is not going as planned or you want to elevate your mood, then simply begin to change the way you are thinking. Look for the good – it is there. Here is an example of what I'm talking about. Let's take a look at Nancy's situation. Nancy and her family were anticipating a well-needed vacation. A break from all the hustle and bustle. This was planned a year ago. The whole family was full of excitement anticipating how much fun they were going to have together. However, when the family arrived at their destination, they were devastated to discover that the weather forecast for most of the vacation was going be rainy. This was due to a passing storm. Nancy and her husband invested so much time and money – she wanted everything to go perfectly. Nancy's three children were very much looking forward to riding on the paddleboats, building sandcastles on the beach, and eating smores by the firepit. They were all bummed out by the unfortunate forecast. Breakfast the next morning became an ongoing conversation about what they were hoping to do. The mood just became more and more somber. After listening to her kids whine all morning long, Nancy and her husband knew they had to do something to survive the next four days with their children. As they walked up to their hotel room it became clear to Nancy what the solution was. She stopped, took a moment, and began to look at things differently. She thought to herself, *We could play board games, go shopping, visit a unique museum – no, it's not what we originally planned, but it could still be enjoyable.* She realized how fortunate she was just to be together with her family and that everyone was healthy. Nancy decided that the inclement weather was not going to ruin her family's beach vacation; instead, she took a second look and embraced it.

Despite whatever you're going through at the moment, stop and think about all your blessings. If you have food in your refrigerator, clothes on your back, a roof over your head, and a place to sleep, you are richer than seventy-five percent of the world. If you have money in the bank or in your wallet, and some spare change, you are among eighty percent of the world's most wealthy people. If you woke up this morning with more health than illness, you are blessed. Take a deep breath in and out, and take a moment to realize how blessed you truly are.

Another way to practice gratitude is to keep a gratitude journal. In your journal, maintain a practice of writing down five things a day that you are grateful for, and try to record a variety. Jot down what you are thankful for no matter how big or small. You'll be surprised that this brings to light how fortunate you are. For example, you may be thankful for a warm cup of coffee in the morning, a hug from your child, indoor plumbing, or a wave from a neighbor. Your blessings don't have to be a lavish vacation or a brand-new car. Savor and absorb the good things that happen all around you. Deepak Chopra says, "When you focus on the things you are grateful for, you go into the source of abundance." In other words, focusing on all that you have, and not what is missing, creates room for more in your life. Gratitude opens your heart and allows you to receive more goodness. A simple thank-you note, phone call, or even a text message sent to a loved one expresses appreciation that will keep you focused on a plentiful life.

When you express gratitude, you are creating an abundance mindset – a belief that there is more of everything, whether that's money, relationships, or opportunities. How does gratitude relate to weight loss, you ask? My simple answer is that it is physics – "like attracts like." When you are coming from a state of abundance, you will attract those circumstances, people, etc. with the same vibration. This is when suddenly you get a text message from a friend who wants to go walking or you receive a healthy delicious recipe that is easy to make. Remember, there are no coincidences. By writing in a gratitude journal, or expressing appreciation, you will establish a firm gratitude habit, which will shift your thinking and create better health and more happiness in your life.

## Self-Talk

No matter how big or small your goal is, there are going to be times when you feel doubtful. Weight-loss attainment is no different. Thoughts may creep up, like: *I'm too old, it takes too long, I don't have what it takes, my mother struggled with weight loss, so that it means...*

Well, I am here to tell you that there is an antidote for that called "self -talk." Your inner voice is filled with all kinds of unspoken words, ranging from negative to positive. Your work is to stay focused on the positive, as doing so will increase your self-confidence and reduce the unnecessary chatter that may impede your progress.

During doubtful times in my weight-loss journey, I retreated to a phrase in a book my mother used to read me as a child, called *The Little Engine That Could*. In the story, any time the train doubted itself and thought it wouldn't make it up the big hill, the train would say, "I think I can, I think I can." You can pretty much figure out that the train succeeded. Therefore, like the train climbing a hill, I just keep on saying to myself, "I know I can, I know I can."

Positive self-talk is a tool that assists you in taking control of your life. You can't build without the right tools. When I was younger, I thought people who talked to themselves were crazy; ironically, it's just the opposite – self-talk is proven to be healthy for us. It works! Self-talk puts you back on track, keeping your goal in sight. I invite you to try it when oppositional thoughts enter your mind. Yes, positive self-talk is pretty much that simple.

Have a positive mindset and keep focused on your goal. No one is a better cheerleader for you than yourself! Keep climbing that hill – you will reach the top. How we talk to ourselves and perceive our situations, in fact, becomes our reality. So again, we have a choice. If we love and appreciate ourselves, life can be wonderful!

# Chapter 13: Give Yourself Permission

*"Balance isn't something you achieve someday."*

– Nick Vujicic

I want you to understand that your decision to lose weight is not a destination; instead, it is a journey. There will be times when you feel balanced and things are going well, and other times…well, not so much. Know that this is all part of the process. You are human and experiencing life with all its surprises. The important thing to remember is to be kind and compassionate to yourself, which is the practice of self-love. It means loving yourself unapologetically. So, the next time you're in yoga class and notice halfway through the class that you're wearing your yoga pants inside out, laugh to yourself – appreciating the fact that you showed up to class. This is an example of being kind to yourself instead of feeling disappointed. Self-love is about acceptance. Self-care, although similar, is more about creating space, making an intentional effort to feel good. We need both to maintain balance in our busy lives.

Let's face it, we all get busy with school, family, and work. It feels as though we get pulled in a million different directions. When this happens, the first thing that seems to go is self-care. It so easily can be pushed aside until you feel you "have time." However, you will never "have time." Instead, you have to make self-care a priority. Build it into your daily practice. For example, you can make self-care part of your morning routine. Self-care along with practicing gratitude were the game changers for me. Read carefully. Without self-care, I would not have been able to sustain my optimal weight. Yes, it is a priority in my life now. Before, I was busy pleasing and filling other people's needs. I forgot about mine! Does this at all sound familiar? You need to schedule time for yourself. One way I make sure I fill my tank for the day is to go through my morning routine. It actually begins the night before by getting to bed between 9:30 and 10 o'clock so that I can get up early enough the next morning without feeling tired. If I wake up before my husband, I let Bella outside to do her "business." From there I head to my mat and practice yoga (sometimes still in my pajamas). After yoga, I meditate. When I finish, I make a cup of freshly brewed coffee, taking a moment to appreciate the aroma before heading to my computer. *Oh yeah,* somewhere in the midst of my morning, I greet my husband with a hug and kiss. I find a morning routine makes me excited for my busy day during the week.

Self-care means intentionally setting aside time for yourself. Self-care does not mean scrolling mindlessly through Facebook or your Instagram feed. It doesn't mean getting your nails done while answering texts or trying to squeeze in an exercise class at night, only to find it keeps you up at night. You see, both exercise and a manicure/pedicure can be forms of self-care for some people, while doing the same activities can be a job to be checked off for another person. It is what you make it. Choose an activity that rejuvenates you and brings you joy.

Taking care of yourself means to nurture and refuel yourself at a deep level, making you whole. As I mentioned, this looks different for each person, so keep in mind that there are many ways to nurture yourself – eating nutritious meals, getting massages, sex, writing, getting a new haircut, exercising, reading, going out to dinner, having coffee with a friend, practicing yoga, or taking an online class. What fills you up?

I can't emphasize the importance of "me time" enough. You can't fake this; just thinking positive thoughts is not enough, rather, taking care of yourself requires taking action. No, self-care is not selfish or self-indulgent. There is no need to feel guilty. On the contrary, your intention to refuel will allow you to be productive. When your tank is full, not on empty, it will resonate with the people around you. When you feel good, these feelings will spill over into your relationships with others. When you routinely practice self-care, you will show up and serve willingly because you feel renewed instead of resentful. You will most likely be able to tackle work obligations with ease rather than feeling anxious. When self-care is part of your routine, your busy schedule becomes exciting rather than burdensome. Remember, your goal is to be healthier, whole, and vigorous.

Now that you have developed good habits, what will you do when life gets out of balance? You know when this begins to happen, as you feel overwhelmed. When you notice this, you must stop and practice self-care – the act of doing for yourself to regain balance. We already talked about eating well, getting enough sleep, and moving as part of the recipe for weight loss, but there are many ways in which you can treat yourself to self-care to feel new again. Know that we are all individuals; diet and lifestyle needs look different for everyone. One person may have the need to get together for dinner with several friends, while other people may enjoy the company and conversation of a good friend over lunch. Self-care is no different.

Self-love is about being compassionate and kind to yourself. It is how you will maintain your natural weight. Yes, schedule time into your week – every week – just for yourself. If you can schedule this time daily, that is even better! Many of us think that if we just work harder, we will achieve our goals. Yes, discipline is definitely a factor in achieving a goal, but it needs to be balanced with self-care. When you take time for yourself, you will have more energy to do what needs to be done. Self-care is synonymous with being healthy; you can't just run five miles a day and eat your greens. There is more to it. Take ownership of your needs. Self-care is the secret sauce to a successful weight-loss journey.

# Chapter 14: Happy Ever After

*"Happiness is your birthright. Claim it!"*

– Gabrielle Bernstein

In Chapter 1, you met Stephanie, who often felt discouraged because she was unable to sustain the diets she implemented. As a result, she lost her confidence and began to feel "less than." However, intuitively she knew there was more, and so she didn't throw in the towel. Stephanie decided to try to improve her body image one more time. She took a holistic approach to losing weight, found the support she needed, and made the difference she was looking for.

You see, your health goes beyond the food you eat and the exercise you do. You can't just swallow a "magic diet pill." It simply does not work that way, even though these are the messages we get from the dieting industry. The Institute of Integrated Nutrition says, "What nourishes you is often not what you put on your plate." Being healthy also means being in alignment with your career, relationships, finances, environment, and spiritual practices. When you are out of balance, it will show up in your body. Yes, in the form of weight gain! Your body is a perfect machine. A fluctuation in weight is a message that something deeper is going on that needs your attention. In this book, you learned ways in which you can regain balance and manage stress. Living with chronic stress shouldn't be the new norm. Living unhappily is not a way to go through life.

This happened to Stephanie – her life was out of balance. She learned the importance of creating space in her day to take care of herself. She now practices meditation each morning, claiming it is "her time." She makes sleep a priority, as she found she needs her eight hours a night to feel refreshed in the morning and tackle her busy day. Stephanie also made a few adjustments to what, and how, she was eating, but could easily manage it because she didn't have to deprive herself of the foods she enjoyed. She feels more in control of what she is eating without rushing through meals like she was used to. Through eating mindfully, she listens to what her body needs. There is no longer a need to follow a restrictive diet. Stephanie developed an exercise routine that she enjoys, yoga, and it also has become part of her self-care.

Stephanie feels better, not just because she found a way to maintain her weight loss, but because she is aligned with who she is on the inside. Her journey was more than just the loss of twenty pounds; Stephanie was really looking for more energy and to be present for herself and her family. She looks and feels younger, and because of all the inner work, her confidence has grown as well. Now, Stephanie realizes how silly she is comparing herself to her sister; the idea that she had to look like Meg dissolved. After all, they have two different body types, and everybody is unique! What works for one may not work for another. Stephanie learned that all she has to do is run her own race and not worry about anyone else's. Stephanie built up the courage to have a heart-to-heart discussion with Meg about how she made her feel inferior growing up. This is also another reason why Stephanie's weight gain affected her so much. Meg also realized that in order not to create a wedge between Stephanie and herself, she had to stop being so judgmental. As a result, the two sisters have a better relationship. They both had a wonderful time at the wedding.

The most exciting piece to the journey is that Stephanie realized she might want to venture out from her longtime teaching career. There was always a little voice in her head that whispered to her about being an author, specifically writing children's books, and the voice only seems to be getting louder and louder. She isn't sure how she will accomplish this goal just yet, but she has faith that she can figure it out. Stephanie has a message to tell, and what better place than through a children's book, which conveys powerful themes in a simple way. Stephanie already knows what her first subject will be: *believing in yourself.* The thought of her new venture excites her! Yes, Stephanie is welcoming her second act.

Friends, my wish for you is that you, like Stephanie, will use the framework I provided in this book to take care of yourself and to look and feel your best. I want you to have a healthy mind and body so that you find joy in doing the work you were born to do. There is a reason you chose to read this book; there are no coincidences. Your inner voice is telling you there is something greater for you to step into. Evolution is inevitable – you just have to be open to it. Resistance to this change will show up in your body through aches and pains, sickness and weight gain; notice the imbalance. What is it telling you? If you are still unsure, then you must get quiet, and the stillness will lead you in the right direction. Too many of us rush through life, unaware of the subtle nudges – messages we are given along the way. I want you to take your life back and enjoy it!

Believe me, I don't live in a world of unicorns and rainbows. *Happy ever after* does not mean that everything is going to go your way all the time. I think it is safe to say we have all been living on earth long enough to know this. It means when faced with disappointment, defeat, doubt, rejection, it will not define you or stop you. We are all faced with these challenges and will continue to be. *Happy ever after* means no circumstances, no event, no person or job will ever have a hold on you. Your true power comes from within, and you choose how you will respond to adversity. Like Stephanie, believe there is a way, and you will find it.

## Here's a Recap

Now that you read the book, let's go over the process to make your weight-loss journey successful whether you're looking to lose ten, twenty, thirty, or forty pounds. The first step on your journey to a permanent weight-loss solution is to identify the reason why you want to lose weight. What is calling you to make a change? Yes, you've tried dieting before, but what is motivating you now? Remember, the seed would not have been planted if it wasn't possible for you to be successful. Ask yourself, "What is different this time?" To refresh, consider why your weight loss is so important to you. Then commit to the cause. Once this is established, start feeling the outcome as if it already happened. So, the next step is to imagine how you will look. Visualize yourself entering a room with a big smile on your face, feeling confident, fitting into the clothes you love, and strutting your stuff. You will not do this just because you like the way you look (after all, there are plenty of skinny unhealthy people in the world), but you will walk confidently because you know that how you feel is aligned with who you truly are. You must feel those good feelings and revisit them throughout the process. Thirdly, you want to take action. This can be achieved by using a tool called a SMART goal, as suggested in Chapter 4. Start with a specific, achievable goal. Don't try to tackle it all at once. Bite-size pieces are more manageable. Lastly, you want to

look at areas of your life where you feel out of balance –
sleep, nutrition, physical movement, environment,
finances, relationships, spirituality, self-care, and career.
No one's life is in balance all the time. It's about
progress, not perfection. Let's take a closer look at each.

When did sleeplessness become an epidemic?
Maybe it's due to the proliferation of all the coffee shops,
or the overload of information we receive each day.
Nevertheless, lack of sleep is a problem that impedes your
health in so many ways, including weight loss. Make sure
you get your rest! This step cannot be overlooked.

As we discussed earlier, there are over a hundred
diets you could implement, and you would probably find
some success with them, but let's face it, you can't
deprive yourself of carbs or ice cream forever; sooner or
later, the diet pendulum is going to swing back with a
vengeance. Instead, practice mindful eating. Include
more fruits, vegetables, and whole grains during
mealtimes. This will have the lasting effect on your
waistline that you are looking for. Also, remember that
drinking plenty of water is a simple habit for staying
healthy.

Movement – notice I did not call it "exercise" – is unique for everyone. So, dance, jog, walk, garden, clean your house, or mow the lawn. Most importantly, make sure that you move and enjoy what you are doing so you feel energized after the activity, not drained. It doesn't make sense to start the day with a high-impact exercise and then sit at a desk all day. Whatever you choose, make it part of a consistent routine.

Your home environment plays a vital role in your health and happiness. Check in with your current situation. Is your space comfortable, and does it give you joy? How does your environment make you feel? One person may be okay with a little mess, while it may drive another person crazy. Do you have old stuff that no longer serves you? There are many organizations that will pick up your used items. Create a home environment that you love so that no matter what kind of day you had, you can come home and relax.

Although money is an uncomfortable subject, it does have a bearing on you if you don't have a handle on your finances, so have a plan and a budget. Your finances can easily take over your life. How much can you spend, and how much can you save? With a little work, you can ease your mind and balance your finances. With a positive attitude, it can be a fun activity rather than a stressful one.

What is the current state of your relationships? Are you seeing your friends as much as you would like? Relationships are a huge part of your well-being, as humans have an innate need for human connection. Most of all, take a look at your relationship with yourself. Are you kind and compassionate to yourself? When you're going through a transformation such as losing weight, don't do it alone. Build your tribe. Surround yourself with people who are going to support you.

Who doesn't want to feel competent, creative, and passionate about their career? No one! Think of how much time you spend at work in a lifetime. Most people spend more time with colleagues than with their own family. Therefore, just like a delicious meal, it is natural to want your career to be satisfying. Take time to reflect on where you are in terms of a career. You may not necessarily have to stop what you are doing if you feel unsatisfied, but explore where you could make the necessary changes you need to fit into your current lifestyle and beliefs.

What is more reassuring than knowing that you are part of something much bigger? It's comforting to me to know that difficult situations in my life happen for a reason and it is all part of the grand plan to guide me to my true self. Having a spiritual practice, whether it means taking a long walk, meditating, or attending a weekly service, strengthens your connection with the Divine. Be open to receive. The Universe is working on your behalf.

Now, let's remember that we are all humans, which means in order to be successful we have to be comfortable with the fact that we are all imperfect creatures. Naturally, unexpected events will arise, however, you will be better equipped to tackle these situations if you take care of yourself. I can't stress enough how important self-care is to your overall health and how it affects others around you. Intentionally plan self-care into your day, especially when you get busy, because this is when you are more apt to forgo it.

I have the belief that we are all here on Earth at this specific time to do great things. The power is within all of us. The choice is ours to take action. The question to ask yourself is, "Do I remain comfortable and complain about what I am not doing, or do I step out of my comfort zone and transition into the work that I am here to do?" It all starts with being healthy!

I would like to end this book with a quote from the late, great Louise Hay, who was a motivational author and inspirational speaker and wrote over a dozen books throughout her life. I find these simple words always bring me peace and serenity. Louise believed that to become whole and healthy, you must balance your body, mind, and spirit. If you've ever read any of her books or watched her videos, she often states these simple words that I personally find comforting: "All is well." Yes, my friends, it is!

# Acknowledgements

Of course, I have to thank my beautiful daughter, Sophia. I love the lessons parents learn from their own children. The one in particular that stands out to me is when you tell me not to worry so much – everything is fine. You are right! I am truly blessed to have you in my life. Never stop chasing your dreams. I love you with all my heart.

I would like to acknowledge my Mom, who always instilled in me the importance of good health from a young age. Many ideas from this book have her name written all over them. To my Dad, who always encouraged me to read. I still enjoy listening to your recap of the latest novel you read. I am amazed by the fact that you still read a book a week.

I want to thank my dear lifelong neighborhood friends. I never realized what a special gift it was to belong to a young tribe just a short walk away. We laughed together, cried together, and dreamed together. I always smile when I think of my childhood.

To my colleagues. Over the last twenty-five years, I have worked with some of the most creative, caring, hardworking people. Teachers do change lives. I see it every day.

This book would not have been created without the education I received from the Institute of Integrated Nutrition – thank you for helping me reach optimal health by making adjustments to both my diet and lifestyle. This inner journey unleashed the passion that compels me to share what I've learned with others.

Lastly, a special thanks to Dr. Angela Lauria and her talented staff at the Author Incubator. Through grace and inspiration, you led me to find my inner author.

# About the Author

Lisa Airhart is a longtime educator. She has expanded her passion from teaching children to helping adults become their best selves through personal growth and development. Lisa received her training to become a Health Coach from the Institute of Integrated Nutrition (IIN). She specializes in helping busy men and women lose unwanted pounds and look and feel their best. She lives in Rhode Island with her husband, Michael, daughter Sophia (when home from college), and beloved dog, Bella. She likes to keep active by practicing yoga, riding her bike, skiing, and taking walks. Lisa enjoys cooking meals for her family and friends and hanging out in her backyard.

# Thank You

To all my readers, thank you for reading. My hope for you is that this book serves as a source for inspiration and guidance so that you are supported through your weight-loss transformation.

To me, personal growth is very exciting. This is why I first became a teacher and now love being a health coach. A health coach is a supportive mentor – the secret sauce to personal growth – because a coach is a guide, on your side, listening attentively to "you." A coach lovingly nudges you toward your goal and supports you during the process. As a holistic health coach, I create a personal plan with you to make you feel your best through food and lifestyle changes. There are simple ways you can optimize your life, and I can get you there. If you are serious about making a change, I can help! You can contact me at for a free consultation at lisaairharthc@gmail.com or by going to lisaairhart.com.

Health and Happiness,

*Lisa*

This book was inspired by my experience at the Institute for Integrative Nutrition® (IIN), where I received my training in holistic wellness and health coaching.

IIN offers a truly comprehensive Health Coach Training Program that invites students to deeply explore the things that are most nourishing to them. From the physical aspects of nutrition and eating wholesome foods that work best for each individual person, to the concept of Primary Food – the idea that everything in life, including our spirituality, career, relationships, and fitness contributes to our inner and outer health – IIN helped me reach optimal health and balance. This inner journey unleashed the passion that compels me to share what I've learned and inspire others.

Beyond personal health, IIN offers training in health coaching, as well as business and marketing. Students who choose to pursue this field professionally complete the program equipped with the communication skills and branding knowledge they need to create a fulfilling career encouraging and supporting others in reaching their own health goals.

From renowned wellness experts as Visiting Teachers to the convenience of their online learning platform, this school has changed my life, and I believe hit will do the same for you. I invite you to learn more about the Institute for Integrative Nutrition and explore how the Health Coach Training Program can help you transform your life. Feel free to contact me to hear more about my personal experience at lisaairhart.com to learn more.

Made in the USA
Columbia, SC
02 August 2020